What to Tell the Kids About Your Divorce

Darlene Weyburne, B.C.D., C.S.W., A.C.S.W.

New Harbinger Publications

Publisher's Note

Distributed in the U.S.A. by Publishers Group West; in Canada by Raincoast Books; in Great Britain by Airlift Book Company, Ltd.; in South Africa by Real Books, Ltd.; in Australia by Boobook; and in New Zealand by Tandem Press.

Copyright © 1999 by Darlene Weyburne
New Harbinger Publications, Inc.
5674 Shattuck Avenue
Oakland, CA 94609

Cover design by Lightbourne Images
Edited by Donna Latte
Text design by Michele Waters

Library of Congress Catalog Card Number: 98-68748
ISBN 1-57224-133-0 Paperback

Printed in the United States of America

New Harbinger Publications' Website address: www.newharbinger.com

01   00   99

10   9   8   7   6   5   4   3   2   1

First printing

This book is dedicated to the children of divorce who courageously struggle to understand what is happening in their lives and to their parents, whose commitment to helping their children and rebuilding their families inspired me to write this book.

I appreciate the experience and knowledge that the staff at Family and Children's Service of Midland, Michigan shared with me. In particular I would like to thank Ginnie Hough, Carole Aulph, Jeanette Obermiller, Sharon Mortensen, and Kristi Mercer for the valuable feedback they gave me.

A sister is a forever friend. Thanks to my sisters, my parents and the rest of my family who loved and supported me throughout my research and writing. Thanks to my niece, Letitia, who so openly shared her feelings with me. Special thanks go to my children, Joshua and Jessica Weyburne, and to my husband and best friend Pat, whose loyalty and commitment has helped me believe that marriage can be a positive growth experience.

Contents

A Special Note from the Author   ix

Introduction   1

1 **How, What, and When to Tell Your Children**   5
About the Divorce
Using a Family Meeting Plan • Trial Separations

2 **Parenting Time (Visitation)**   17
How to Determine the Schedule for Parenting Time •
Where Should Parents and Children Live? • Guidelines
for Making the Transition Between Homes Easier • What
to Do During Your Parenting Time • Family Pets •
Long-Distance Parenting • When a Parent Doesn't Visit

3 **Parenting Rules**   35
How to Write Clear, Reasonable, and Enforceable Rules

4 **Coparenting**   41
Developing Respect for the Other Parent • Supporting
Your Children's Relationship With the Other Parent •
Communicating with Each Other • Child Support

5 **Communicating More Effectively**   51
How to Use "I" Messages • Keep the Kids Out of the
Middle • Keep Communication with Your Children
Open • Spend Time Individually with Each of Your
Children • Listen to Your Children • Ask Your Children
to List Questions and Concerns About the Divorce •

Teach Your Children How to Express Feelings
Appropriately • Continue to Hold Weekly Family
Meetings • Normalize Your Children's Lives

6 Understanding and Helping Your Children   **71**
Express Their Feelings
Children's Stages of Grief • Typical Feelings Experienced
by Children of Divorce • Role Model Appropriate
Expression of Feelings • Building Self-Esteem

7 Age-Specific Reactions to Divorce   **89**
Birth to One Year: The Age of Trust • Ages One to
Three: The World Revolves Around Them • Ages Three
to Five: The Age of Curiosity • Ages Six to Eight: The
Age of the Loose Tooth • Ages Nine to Twelve: The
Age of Accomplishment • Ages Thirteen to Eighteen:
The Age of Raging Hormones • Adult Children of
Divorce: What Do I Want to Do?

8 When You're Ready to Start Dating Again   **107**
What to Look For in a Partner • When a Relationship
Becomes Serious

9 Remarriage   **115**
Before You Get Married • What Makes a Marriage Work

10 Stepparenting   **123**
Developing Relationships Between Stepchildren and
Stepparents • Financial Issues • Developing Your
Parenting Skills • The Role of an Extended Family

11 Taking Care of Yourself   **137**
Reducing Your Stress • Ten Healthy Habits to Handle
Stresst • Building Your Self-Esteem

12 Confronting and Coping with Your Feelings   **155**
The Seven Psychological Tasks of Divorce • Changing
Your Negative Thinking

13 Therapy   **175**
Therapy for Your Children • Do I Need a Therapist? •
Finding a Qualified Therapist

Afterword   **187**

References, Bibliography, and Additional Reading   **191**

Personal Notes and To Do Lists   **195**

A Special Note
from the Author

Just after completing this book, I was diagnosed with breast cancer. My first thought was, "This can't be happening." My first question was, "What do I tell my kids?" As I struggle with the pain and emotional roller coaster of my illness, I realize, more than ever, that divorcing parents have similar thoughts and face similar struggles.

Just before being diagnosed with cancer, my eleven-year-old son and I had been engaged for several months in a major power struggle over who was in control of the house. I worried that he, like many children of divorce, would blame himself for having dramatically increased my stress level and therefore somehow causing my illness. My eight-year-old daughter reacted by jumping away from me and asking if she could catch it. This reminded me of how teenagers worry about their ability to have happy healthy relationships, given their parents' inability to make the marriage work.

When my husband took the kids skiing, I felt the same ambivalence divorced parents feel when their children are having fun with the other parent. I was overjoyed that they could enjoy this time together and build a stronger relationship. Yet part of me resented and grieved that I could not be with them to share this joy and that what little energy I did have was spent making sure they did their homework and chores.

When my son asked me if I was afraid, I, like divorcing parents, had to stop myself from expressing the intense terror I experienced. Yet I needed to help him accept that the fear, anger, and sadness we were both experiencing was normal and that it was okay to express these feelings. I know that like me, divorcing parents worry that their anger, depression, guilt, and fear will interfere with their ability to assist their children in coping with the trauma they are experiencing—and that often we don't even realize that we are doing this.

I, like you, never dreamed that at this stage in my life I would be going through this crisis. But I believe that with hard work and support from family, friends, and a few professionals, you and I and our children will not only survive but will learn and grow out of this experience, and that we will appreciate and make full use of the precious little time we have to be with and teach our children.

Introduction

My German grandfather was born on the edge of the twentieth century. During his lifetime, he saw his homeland torn in two by the building of the Berlin wall. When I was a child, he used to talk about how children and parents risked their lives to cross over this wall to be reunited with each other. In 1989, I cried as I watched the wall being torn down and Germany struggle to rebuild itself, remembering the families who had lost their lives and knowing that my grandfather was not alive to witness it. Families going through a divorce often feel that they are in a war zone. Their lives are being ripped apart and walls between family members are erected. Parents who are battle weary and overwhelmed by their emotional reaction to the divorce need assistance in helping their children through this conflict. My hope for the coming century is that we give parents this support and that in a crisis we focus on rebuilding families rather than building walls.

Nearly half of all children born in this country in the last decade will live through their parents' divorce. This represents over one million children every year who, after reaching adulthood, have a greater risk of experiencing troubled relationships with the opposite sex and are more likely to become divorced themselves. Children of divorce have more behavioral problems, more difficulties with authority figures, and lower academic achievement. Divorce can be the most devastating experience of your children's lives because it disrupts their developing sense of trust, security, self, and where they fit into family and other groups. In her ten-year study of divorce, Judith Wallerstein found that three out of five children interviewed felt rejected by at least one of their parents. Almost half of the children she talked to became "worried, underachieving, self-deprecating and sometimes angry adults" (Wallerstein and Kelly 1980).

There are, however, specific steps you can take that can minimize the social and emotional damage to your children's growth and development and help all of you successfully rebuild your and your children's lives. In her review of the current research literature regarding children whose parents had divorced, Joan Kelly concluded that for children who live in marriages characterized by frequent and intense conflict, "... the divorce may promote more positive adjustment over the long term, particularly if the parents reduce their conflict or work their disputed issues out in counseling or mediation and avoid placing their children in the middle" (Kelly 1998). Judith Wallerstein notes that children "... who did well were helped along the way by a combination of their own inner resources and supportive relationships with one or both parents, grandparents, stepparents, siblings, or mentors [and] ... benefited from the continued relationship with two good parents who—despite their anger and disappointment with each other—were able to cooperate in the tasks of childbearing" (Wallerstein 1989). This book teaches you the steps you can take to accomplish this. It will walk you through the entire process, from telling your children that you are divorcing to successfully coparenting and stepparenting. It will tell you how your divorce will affect your children and how you can ease their unhappiness.

The English philosopher Herbert Spencer said, "The great aim of education is not knowledge but action."

This book is not just an explanation of how divorce affects children. If you're a parent going through divorce, you have already begun to see how the divorce is affecting your children. This book is aimed at helping you take the necessary *action* to help your children. To get the most out of this book, do not just read it. This book is designed to be a workbook; the learning process takes place as you do the work. Keep a pen with you as you read and complete the exercises or instructions as you go. When the text tells you to do something, stop reading and follow the instructions. You may be tempted to skip these parts with the intention of going back later to fill them in. However, intentions don't produce results, actions do. So take action now and, before reading further, go to the section at the end of this book labeled Personal Notes and To Do Lists and write down what you would like to accomplish with the completion of this book.

Parents at various stages in their divorce process will benefit from reading the entire book even though some sections may not seem relevant at first glance. For example, chapter 1 focuses on when and how to tell your children about the divorce. If you have already told your children about the divorce, you can still benefit from using the Family Meeting Plan exercise in that chapter to help your children understand why you are divorcing, help them talk about their feelings and concerns, and assure them that they are still loved.

As a cognitive behavioral therapist, I have found that often, much of the work in therapy is done *between* sessions. I use sessions to practice skills that my clients are developing and give them homework that enables them to utilize what they are learning. Giving them homework also communicates to my clients that I believe that they are capable of making the changes necessary to accomplish their goals.

The exercises in this book can be used as homework assignments; various chapters can be studied that pertain to the individual issues you are working on. Treatment plans can be written (with your therapist, if you are seeing one) to incorporate these exercises. For example, a long-term goal for your family could be to facilitate cooperation between you and your former partner. The short-term goal would be for you and the other parent to complete the Creating a School Folder exercise in chapter 4 in two weeks. Ask your therapist to discuss with you obstacles that may interfere with successful completion of this assignment. You may need assistance in identifying how completion of the exercises is consistent with the goals you have set for yourself and your children.

The information and advice in this book is a combination of seventeen years of postgraduate clinical experience and research. I have used, in part, the data that Judith Wallerstein collected in her longitudinal study on the effects of divorce as a basis for my age-specific descriptions in chapter 8.

The examples and quotes used in this book are amalgams of the stories that families have shared with me. I have created and altered actual accounts and changed names and ages to assist the reader in understanding the material presented and to protect the clients' confidentiality.

1

How, What, and When to Tell Your Children About the Divorce

KEY POINTS

- Tell your children you are divorcing.
- Tell them together, before one of you moves out.
- Plan ahead of time what you will say to them about the divorce.
- Without blaming the other parent, be direct, honest, and open.
- Allow time to talk about the divorce and answer questions.
- Reassure your children that they will still see both parents, if that is the case.
- Help them understand that the divorce is not their fault.
- Communicate that you still love them.

Dear Mom and Dad,

There is something going on and I wish you would tell me what it is. Instead I am left assuming that you are getting a divorce. Are you separating because you got in a fight or a combination of fights, is there another person, are you falling out of love, or is it me? Have I done something wrong? You haven't told me otherwise, so I am just assuming. Do you think I don't hear the yelling, crying, and slamming doors? I notice the newspapers with red circles around "apartment for rent" and the blankets on the couch when I get up in the morning. You may be trying to protect me, but what are you protecting me from? My imagination can think of things far worse than what you can tell me. I'm hurt and frustrated. I wish you would tell me what is going on. You may think it is easier not to tell me, but I obviously already know something. You are hurting me more by not telling me the truth. Please, what is happening to our family?

Love, Letitia

How you and your former partner handle the initial separation will affect how well your children adjust. Set aside intense feelings toward your spouse and focus on what your children need. If you fail to do this, any destructive behavior that ended your marriage can continue to destroy your children. Although it may be difficult for you, your children need for you and their other parent to talk to them about the divorce. Talking to your children in a neutral manner is a key ingredient in the healing process.

Jason's preschool teacher had called his mother because Jason, age five, had been banging his head on the floor yelling, "bad, bad," for the past week. Last week, Jason's father had moved out. His parents felt he was too young to understand, so they had chosen not to tell Jason about the divorce. When his teacher had talked to Jason about it he said, "I broke Daddy's car and now he's gone." After talking to his mother, the teacher learned that the morning his father left, Jason had pulled his father's favorite model car off the shelf and it had shattered when it hit the floor. Not telling Jason why his father had moved out had resulted in Jason thinking that his dad was mad at him and that it was his fault that his dad had left.

Keep in mind that children are not spectators in divorce, they are participants. They need to be told about it. It is your responsibility, as a parent, to explain to your children the decision to divorce. Failure to talk about the impending divorce can be emotionally and socially damaging to your children. Most children know a lot more about what is going on in their home than parents think they do. Your children hear you when you don't think that they are listening. They hear parents fighting, they know if mom is sleeping in the spare bedroom, and they listen more closely when parents whisper behind closed doors. Children can also sense emotional tension between parents. They are often aware that the silence between parents signifies conflict. Children sense that you are upset even when you say that everything is fine—your actions, facial expressions, and tone of voice may communicate something other than what you are saying verbally. Not telling your children you are divorcing may intensify their trauma, isolate them further, or, as in Jason's case, cause them to blame themselves for your unhappiness.

After being separated for over a year, Bill filed for divorce. He was tired of fighting with his wife every time he came to the house, and wanted to get on with his life. Their youngest son John, age nine, was having trouble in school and had been suspended for fighting. Mary, fifteen, had just quit the school basketball team and had been spending more and more time alone in her room. Their oldest son Matt, a freshman at the state university, had not been home to visit for five months. Sue felt as though her family was falling apart and didn't want to add to her children's problems by telling them about the divorce, but after several heated arguments she agreed to tell them. Together, Bill and Sue sat down and planned what to say. Although it had been difficult, planning ahead helped Sue and Bill stay calm and focus on the children. They waited until their oldest son was home on college break so that they could tell the family together. The children handled the news better than Sue expected. Initially, they were very upset. Matt just left and went back to school. Mary locked herself in her room and refused to come out. John broke the Pinewood Derby car that he and his dad had built together. However, three months later Sue felt the talk had actually improved their communication. Matt had been calling home more frequently and was able to tell his mother how sick he was of listening to them fight. John and his dad had fixed the car and John was able to talk about how angry he was. Mary was able to talk about how much she missed playing basketball as a family. Both Bill and Sue agreed that, although it had been difficult, the family meeting had opened communication and helped their children adjust to the divorce.

Using a Family Meeting Plan

When a decision is made to divorce or separate, tell the other parent that the two of you should tell the children together. Before one of you moves out, set up a day, time, and place to talk about how the two of you will tell your children. Plan a family meeting to help you communicate to your children what is happening. Discuss with the other parent what you plan to say. Think carefully about what you will say and how this will affect your children's future emotional adjustment. What you say may change during the discussion but planning ahead can help decrease your anxiety and allow you to be more neutral.

During your meeting with the other parent and while communicating with your children, practice positive communication through the use of "I" messages. "I" messages involve clearly speaking in the here and now, in a nonjudgmental tone of voice. "I" messages relay feelings and target a specific idea. Sam, father of triplets, approached his children's mother by saying, "I am concerned about how our divorce will affect our children. I would like to talk to you about what we will say to the children before one of us moves out." ("I" messages are discussed in more detail in chapter 5.)

Prior to holding a family meeting, read through this chapter and the next. Complete Exercise 1, which will help you plan what to say.

EXERCISE 1: FAMILY MEETING PLAN

Date of Meeting:

Time of Meeting:

Location of Meeting:

1. Have the following supplies on hand: pad of paper, pens, a big desk calendar, and facial tissues.

2. Each parent should express love for the children.

3. Explain that you will be talking and listening to them for about the next hour. Tell them, "This meeting is important. We will not answer the door or phone during the meeting."

4. If this is a trial separation, tell your children that. Later on, if you decide to divorce, you will need to have another family meeting to tell them that you are proceeding with the divorce.

5. Write down your explanation of why you are getting a divorce. During the meeting, use this explanation to inform your children why you are divorcing.

"Your Mom/Dad and I are getting divorced because,

_____

_____

_____

_____

(You may need to work on this before it feels right. Read your explanation and ask yourself these questions: Does it sound as if both parents are taking responsibility for the divorce? Does it focus on the parents and not on the children?

If the answer to either question is no, rework your explanation.)

6. Again, each parent should express love for each child.

7. State who will be moving out, when that will happen, and where the parent will be living. Draw a map to show where that location is. Include the address and phone number, and give each child a copy.

8. Explain the initial parenting time schedule. Mark on the calendar when your children will be with each parent and show it to them. Use one color to highlight time with Dad and another color to highlight time with Mom. Tell the children where you will be posting this calendar. Some families call this the Family Calendar and use it to list all other family

activities such as doctor and dentist appointments, sporting events, and school functions.

Or, if you have decided to have the children stay in the home with the parents taking turns moving in and out, explain that at this time and mark on the calendar the dates each parent will be home.

9. Each parent should sign the following agreement:

I, out of my commitment to raise emotionally healthy children, agree to communicate to my children the changes that will be happening in our family. I will remain focused on their needs during this meeting.

Mother: _____

Father: _____

When Is the Best Time to Tell Them?

Carol, age forty-eight, was furious with her husband, Joe, who had, without telling her ahead of time, left the state with his twenty-two-year-old receptionist. "I don't know what I was more angry about, him having the affair or his moving out and leaving me to explain it to the kids. What I felt like doing was putting the kids on a plane and letting him and his bimbo explain what had happened. Instead, I called my best friend and unloaded on her. After I cooled off I got all the kids together, told them how much I loved them, and explained that their dad and I were getting a divorce."

Tell your children about the divorce during a family meeting, before either parent moves out. Telling them at a preplanned meeting helps your children understand that the parents have discussed and reached this decision themselves and not because of any bad behavior that the child may have exhibited that day. The meeting should occur a few days before one parent moves out. The entire family should be present. If one of you has already moved out, that person should still come back to hold the meeting. However, if the other parent refuses to attend, hold the meeting without him or her. Again, set aside a minimum of one hour for this meeting, but do not let it run much longer. (This is especially true if you have young children who have a limited attention span.) You may need to end the meeting before everyone has had a chance to say what they need to say. If this happens, communicate to your children that their feelings and concerns are important and set up a specific date and time to continue the discussion. Be direct, honest, and open. Avoid using this meeting to ventilate feelings toward the other parent or blame him or her for the divorce. This may be very difficult for you because you have not yet had time to deal with your feelings. It helps to keep in mind that staying neutral is crucial for your children's future adjustment. During the initial and future meetings, stay focused on the agreement that you and the other parent signed.

Tell older children ahead of time that you will be having this meeting, but give them just enough time to plan around their schedules. Tell younger children just prior to the meeting. Doing so too far in advance may increase their anxiety, particularly if they anticipate the purpose of the meeting. Do not give details about the meeting ahead of time. Let your children know that Mom and Dad have something important to discuss with them and leave it at that. Tell them you will answer their questions at the meeting.

Do not tell your children and do not move out around a major holiday. Telling your children at Christmas, Passover, or near their birthday will forever link these two events in their minds. Holidays are a time to look back and reminisce. Imagine if someone you loved died on Thanksgiving. Every year after that, Thanksgiving becomes a reminder of the grief you experienced over losing that person. Samantha, age sixteen, talked to me about her alcoholic father moving out Christmas day. "Why did he have to leave on Christmas? Every year my friends get all worked up about what they're going to get for Christmas. I hate it. We get out the Christmas decorations and my mom starts crying. I see these stupid Hallmark commercials about families getting together and I feel like throwing up. My friends think about what's going to be under the tree for them. What I think about is seeing my dad's suitcases lined up by the door and my sister hanging on to his leg, begging him not to leave. The truth is, part of me was glad he was leaving, but why did he have to wreck our Christmas?"

Divorce is a loss even for children who wish that their parents would divorce. It is the end of the belief that you are part of a big happy family. Even if your family does not appear to be a happy one, your children may fantasize that someday it will be. The anniversary of the divorce may remind your children of the loss of this fantasy. You can help minimize this loss by choosing an appropriate time to tell your children and by keeping this event separate from happy memories that your children experience.

Right now, give some thought as to when might be the best time to tell your children. Go to the Personal Notes and To Do List at the back of the book and write down when you plan to tell your children about the divorce as well as when one parent will be moving out.

What to Tell Your Children About Your Reasons for Divorce

Sherry was a quiet thirteen-year-old girl who had trouble making friends. She chewed on her fingernails and looked at the floor as she talked about how her dad had told her about the divorce. "My dad told me he was leaving because my mom was a slut and that she was 'whoring' around with Mitch who lived next door. He said he couldn't stand being in this house anymore. How could I face my friends? Everyone always said I looked just like my mom. I knew they would think I was just like her." Children will feel ashamed of themselves if they think that people will see them as bad because of what their parents are doing. You need to tell your children that they have nothing to be ashamed of because they had nothing to do with the divorce. Shame prevented Sherry from reaching out to adults and peers who could have provided the support she needed throughout the divorce.

Help reduce your children's shame by being direct, maintaining eye contact, and giving them an unbiased explanation of why you are divorcing. Don't divulge the specific details of the relationship. It is okay to express your sadness about the divorce; this gives your children permission to morn and cry. But to explain the reason for the breakup, use nonblaming statements such as the following:

- "We don't love each other anymore."

- "We have not been able to work out our differences and problems and cannot be happy living together."

- "When your mom and I got married, we loved each other and we thought we would want to live with each other for the rest of our lives. As we grew older, our feelings, needs, likes, and dislikes began to change and we grew apart. We couldn't agree on things or get along with each other. Living together has become more and more difficult and we are both very unhappy. We now realize that our marriage no longer works and we have decided to get a divorce. Having children has been the best part of our marriage and we both love all of you."

- "Your dad and I have been trying to work out our problems for a long time. We now realize that we cannot do this and have decided to get a divorce. This has been a very hard decision and we are very sad about it. We are sorry that we have hurt you. We will continue to take care of you, but it will be from two separate homes. We both love you and will do our best to help all of you adjust to the divorce."

When I am explaining divorce to children, I will often ask them who their best friend was or what their favorite game or activity was three years ago. I then ask them who their best friend is now or what is now their favorite game or activity. If these two things are different, I talk to them about how people change and how their parents changed and grew apart.

Keep in mind the developmental stages that your children are at and their intellectual understanding of the information you give them (chapter 7 describes age-specific reactions to divorce). When my sister was going through her divorce, my son, who was five at the time, asked me if I was going to get married again. I was afraid that he thought since Aunt Chris was getting a divorce that meant I was too. I went into a twenty minute explanation of how his dad and I had promised to love each other for the rest of our lives and how we worked hard at staying together. I told him that even though we fought sometimes we tried to work things out and forgive each other. My son patiently waited until I had finished my lecture and then said to me, with a confused look on his face, "No, I want to know if you are going to marry Daddy again. At Aunt Eileen's wedding we got those red cherries in our pop and I want to know when we're going to get them again." Keep your explanation short and simple. Don't give your children more information than they can handle. Don't worry about not giving enough details. If you establish open communication and you fail to provide the specific information that your children are looking for, they will ask more questions. Right now, think about some age-appropriate explanations for your divorce. Turn to the Personal Notes and To Do List at the back of the book and write down your explanation of why you are getting a divorce.

Kirstyn, five, asked her mom, "If you can stop loving Daddy, will you stop loving me too?" Reassure your children that you will always love them. Explain briefly how the love parents have for their children is different from the love a husband and wife have for each other. Explain that the love a parent has for a child will not end. Betty told her eight-year-old daughter, "You and I have the same blue eyes. You have your dad's smile and his sense of humor. You're a part of us and our love for you will never change." Again, give some thought to this and then turn to your Personal Notes and To Do List. Write down your explanation of how your love for your children is different from the love you had for their other parent. Doing this now will help you when the time comes to talk to your children.

Reassure your children that both of their parents still love them and that they will continue to see both of them. Paul told his four-year-old, "Your mom and I no longer love each other but we still love you. We're glad we had you and we will always love and want to be with you." What could you say to your children to assure them that you still love them? Write down your ideas at the back of the book.

When you finish telling your children about the divorce, listening to their concerns, and answering their questions (or if you have gone over an hour), end the meeting. Tell your children you love them and you will continue to listen to their thoughts and feelings about the divorce. Tell them that you will continue to have family meetings and that you expect all of them to attend. Assure them that you will continue to let them know about developments in the divorce process. Stress the importance of their thoughts and feelings and write on the calendar the dates and times for future discussions. This will communicate that you are not avoiding the issue and will reinforce your support of their right to have and express feelings. Say something such as, "Things are going to feel different for a while and it will take all of us time to adjust. If you're confused, don't be afraid to ask questions and let us know how you're feeling. We both love you very much and your thoughts and feelings are important to us." After the meeting, turn to your Personal Notes section at the back of this book and write down anything you weren't able to finish discussing. Include anything that you need to follow up on, either alone with a child or at the next family meeting.

What to Do if the Divorce Is Due to Abondonment, Abuse, or Incarceration

If a parent has abandoned the family and you do not know where he or she is, or if or when the other parent will return, tell your children you do not know. Do not make up elaborate stories about the whereabouts of the other parent. Do not lie or put down the other parent. Explain the fact that the parent has left and you do not know where he or she is living. It is okay to tell your children what action you have taken to find the other parent, such as contacting friends or relatives.

Brent, six, drew a *Star Wars* picture for me. When I asked him about the characters he pointed to Luke Skywalker and said, "That's me." He said his dad was Hans Solo. When I commented that I couldn't see Hans Solo in the picture he said, "The Millennium Falcon is missing but the squadron is out searching for him." Two weeks prior to this, Brent had come home from school to find that his father had, without telling anyone, moved out. Brent's mother did not know where he was. He had been a long-term cocaine addict, and she suspected that he was using again and staying with one of his drug-addicted friends. She told Brent that she did not know where his father was but that she had called Grandma and two of his friends, asking them to call her if they heard from him. When I talked to Brent about how Luke Skywalker felt, Brent expressed sadness. He did not say that Luke was to blame for Hans Solo's disappearance. Knowing that his family and friends (Luke Skywalker's squadron) were trying to find his father helped Brent focus on how these people cared about him rather than on his fear about what was happening to his father.

If you are leaving because of physical abuse, first take action to insure your and your children's safety. If your children have witnessed or have been the victims of this abuse, it is okay to tell them why you have left. Explain that you (and they) cannot continue to live this way. Remember that even in abusive situations, what you say about the other parent will affect how your children feel about themselves.

If your children tell you or you suspect that they are being abused by the other parent, immediately consult with a therapist or child protection service worker. This will assist you in developing a safe plan to appropriately assess and deal with the situation. You can locate people who can help by calling Childhelp USA at 1-800-4-A-CHILD. This is a national child abuse hotline that offers 24 hour a day support to children and adults.

If you are leaving because of child or spouse abuse, alcohol or drug addiction, or the incarceration of your spouse, I encourage you to talk to a professional counselor. (Chapter 13 will assist you in locating a qualified therapist.) If possible and if you are not in danger, consult with this counselor before you talk to your children. If the other parent has an emotional or physical disorder that impairs his or her ability to safely take care of your children, give your children an age-appropriate explanation of this. For example, "Mom has a drug problem. She will be able to see you when she gets the problem under control." Or, "Dad has a problem controlling his temper. When he learns how to express his feelings without hurting anyone, he will be able to visit with you."

Trial Separations

If both parents agree that this is a trial separation, tell your children that Mom or Dad will be moving out on a trial basis. Tell them the purpose of this separation. Let them know what your plans are and where the other parent will be living. Assure them that they will continue to see the other parent. Let them know you will continue to communicate with them about the decisions you and the other parent make that will affect them.

If only one parent is clear that he or she wants a divorce and this parent is moving out, tell your children you are getting a divorce. The parent who does not want the divorce will need to work on his or her feelings about this separately. (Chapter 12 will help you with this.)

2

Parenting Time (Visitation)

KEY POINTS

- Call the time your children spend with you "parenting time" instead of "visitation."
- Your children should not choose whom they live with.
- Develop and stick to a parenting schedule.
- Be on time and don't cancel visits.
- Allow children to share clothes and toys between the two homes, and give them their own space in each home.
- Do not try to compensate for lost time by buying too many gifts or never saying no.
- Allow contact with the other parent during your parenting time.

"I hated the word 'visitation.' It made me feel like I was only a temporary dad or some distant relative" (Aurelo, father of three). Calling the time your children spend with you "parenting time" instead of "visitation" helps normalize the changes that occur due to the divorce. Feeling that they are at home with either parent rather than "just visiting" will enhance your children's feeling of being part of a family.

Spend time with your children as soon as possible after you move out. When Angel's father moved out, he did not see Angel, age three, for two weeks. After spending the day together, Angel said, "I'm glad you still love me, Daddy." Show your children you still love them by seeing them as soon as possible after you move out. This is particularly true for young children who do not have an accurate sense of time.

How to Determine the Schedule for Parenting Time

How much time children spend with each parent varies from family to family. Many families choose to have the children live with one parent during the week and spend one weekday evening and alternate weekends with the other parent. The children then spend alternate holiday and school vacations with each parent. However, there's a great deal of variety in how parents determine parenting time, with many parents spending equal amounts of time with their children. Parents who live in different states sometimes have their children spend summers with one parent and the school year with the other parent. Other families switch every week or every other week. Your work schedules will play a part, as they did for Frances and Carlos. Frances works as a nurse, twelve-hour shifts Friday through Sunday. Carlos works Monday through Friday. Frances picks her children up after school on Mondays and keeps them until Friday morning when they leave for school. Carlos then picks the children up from school on Fridays and keeps them until Monday morning. This way their children do not spend any time in daycare and get to spend a lot of time with both parents.

Parents have to decide what will work best for their family. Keep in mind the ages of the children and which parent was the primary caregiver before the divorce. If young children are used to being put to bed and woken up in the morning by the same parent, it will take time for your children to adjust to the other parent doing these things. Younger children also tend to need more frequent contact with both parents. With older children, consider their schedule of school and social activities when determining the parenting schedule. The important factor to remember is that your children need to spend as much time as possible with both parents, but not to the detriment of their schooling or important activities such as concerts, plays, or school sporting competitions. If, for example, your child has a research paper due or a swim meet is approaching, the child should probably stay for the days leading up to the big day with the parent who is available and willing to transport the child to and from the library or pool. This does not mean, however, that children should work out the parenting schedule—parents, not their children, should develop the schedule. "When Dad asked me, I told him I wanted to live with him. My brother, who was the jock in the family and Dad's favorite, said he wanted to live with Mom. I wanted to live with Mom too, but this was my chance to be Dad's favorite" (Terrance, twelve). Living arrangements and parenting time is an adult decision. Giving children the power to choose with whom they live places them in a no-win situation in which they hurt one of their parents with either choice. It allows your children to use the threat of moving in with the other parent to manipulate both of you. Children do not have the experience or knowledge to decide with whom they should live. They have parents to make those decisions for them. This does not mean that you don't listen to your children's thoughts and feelings about their living situation. If your children say they want to live with the other parent, help them label their feelings and develop strategies to handle difficult situations instead of using moving as the solution. For example, if your child yells, "You never let me do anything. I'm going to go live with Dad!" say, "I know you're angry that

I won't let you go to the party tonight. The next time you want to go to a party, tell me ahead of time so that I can talk to the parents who live there before I make my decision."

It is in your and your children's best interest for you and the other parent to decide together when your children will be with each parent. Usually, the court will support a parenting agreement that the two of you have proposed together. If you cannot come to an agreement, however, the court will decide for you, and the court's decision may not be favorable to either of you. Work with your former partner to decide the parenting time schedule.

Where Should Parents and Children Live?

If parents are comfortable with allowing children to remain in the home and themselves moving in and out, this can be the least stressful situation for the children. Most parents, however, do not find this feasible. Another option that can facilitate your children's adjustment to the divorce is to have both parents live in the same neighborhood. Living close allows your children to walk or ride their bikes to and from both parents' houses. This is also easier for parents because children can go directly to the other parent's house after school rather than having to be chauffeured. "It was hard living so close to my ex. I'd get this pain in the pit of my stomach when I'd run into him at the grocery store or see him driving around with his new girlfriend. But living close gave me a chance to see my kids more. If their dad was working, they would ride their bikes over and we'd sit on the porch and have ice cream. It helped them, too. They could still see their friends when they were with me and they could ride their bikes to school" (Clara, mother of five). Although it can be emotionally difficult to live so close to the other parent, doing so allows you to more fully participate in your children's daily activities.

Anna, age ten, had to move to a new city when her parents divorced. "Not only did I lose my dad in the divorce, when Mom and I moved I had to leave my best friend." If possible, one of the parents should remain in the original home for at least one year. This will help reduce the stress caused by the many changes that occur during a divorce and will allow your children to continue to attend the same school and keep the same friends.

Guidelines for Making the Transition Between Homes Easier

- Clarify when your children will be with each parent.

  Update the calendar that you gave your children at the first family meeting. Make sure you have highlighted the days that your children will spend with Dad in one color and the days they will spend with Mom in another color. Knowing when they will see the other parent again will help give them a sense of stability and assist them in coping with feelings of loss.

- Be consistent and on time for your parenting time.

  "I used to sit on the front porch waiting for my dad to show up for his visit. By the time he got there I was so angry I felt like telling him I didn't want to go. I never did because I also missed him. I was afraid that if I told him how I felt he wouldn't show up at all" (Shantel, ten). Stick to your parenting schedule. Be consistent and on time when picking up and dropping off your children. Guard against canceling visits. Your children take it very personally when you are late or cancel, regardless of your excuse. They feel unimportant and unloved when parents repeatedly are late or cancel visits. The family that your children relied on to always be together no longer exists. Right now your children need something new to trust. They should spend their emotional energy on having fun, doing well in school, being responsible, and establishing positive social skills. They should not be spending their time looking out the window and worrying about why you have not yet shown up for your visit.

  If, on occasion, you are going to be late picking up or dropping off your children, call and tell them and your former partner that you will be late. This will assure your children that you are coming and will help avoid a hostile confrontation in front of their other parent when you arrive.

  Show some flexibility in your children's requests for changes in the schedule. "When I asked my dad if I could switch weekends and go with my mom to our family reunion, he was cool about it. He told me he'd miss me but he hoped I'd have a good time" (Carlata, eleven). On occasion, to accommodate family vacations or special events, the schedule can be altered. Discuss these changes beforehand with everybody concerned.

- Establish two homes.

"The first time I went to stay with my dad after the divorce it felt really weird. He lived in this tiny apartment on the third floor of this old building. But when I saw that he had taken all my baseball trophies and pictures and lined them up on a shelf in my room, it didn't feel so strange" (Luke, twelve). Give your children their own space in each home, and give them a say in how they decorate this space. This can be their own room, bed, closet, dresser drawers, or even, if you have limited space in your home, a bookshelf. Do not disturb or change this space while your children are with the other parent. Allowing your children to leave some clothes, toys, and toiletries at each house will aid them in feeling that both residences are home. Also, having separate clothes and toys at both houses will allow them to fit everything they will need in their backpack instead of having to pack suitcases each time they switch houses. Buying two separate wardrobes will be more expensive but will help normalize the change. You can reduce the cost by sharing more expensive items like winter coats and boots but buying two sets of underwear, socks, and pajamas. In addition, allow children to share favorite clothes and toys between the two homes. Make sure younger children have their special toy or blanket with them each time they leave your home.

Make a checklist of the clothes, toys, personal items, and school supplies that will travel back and forth between the homes. This will help your children organize their things and reduce the stress created by forgotten items. Below is a sample list that should help you get started.

My Personal Kit

School folder
Schoolbooks and any supplies needed to complete homework
Personal books and magazines
Journal or diary
Glasses
Retainer or other medical equipment
Medicine
Sporting equipment for games or practice
Shoes, boots, sandals

Dress clothes
Play clothes
Coats, mittens, hats
Favorite stuffed toy or blanket
Musical instrument and sheet music

Jot down all the items you can think of in the Personal Notes section at the back of the book.

- Tour the new neighborhood.
  "At first I was really mad that we had to move to Midland after the divorce. But when Mom showed me the huge soccer complex near where we would be living, I got kind of excited" (Cecil, eleven). If you do move, take walks through the new neighborhood. Introduce yourself and your children to the neighbors. Find out where the playgrounds are and visit the school. Many schools will allow children to come visit for a day before you move. Depending on your children's interests, show them where the science center, basketball courts, or dance studios are located.

- Avoid conflict with the other parent when dropping off or picking up the children.
  Sophia, ten, was brought to counseling by her father because he was concerned about her behavior when it was time for him to take her back to her mother's at the end of his parenting time. Several hours before it was time to return to her mother's home, Sophia was irritable and oppositional. She complained of stomachaches and would sometimes hole up in her room and refuse to talk to anyone. Sophia's dad contacted me because he was concerned that there was a problem at Mom's house and he was hoping I could help Sophia deal with the divorce. For several weeks I talked to Sophia about her feelings and had her do some drawings and collages of how she saw her family situation. Sophia, who was her parents' only child, told me about how her parents got into a fight every time her dad brought her back from a visit. "Mom would get angry that I forgot my glasses or my gloves or that my dad didn't make me finish my homework. Dad would start yelling back about how Mom hadn't told him I had homework and that it was my responsibility. It made me sick. I dreaded Sunday nights." Sophia enjoyed and loved both of her parents and wanted to be with both of them. She seemed to have accepted the divorce but felt torn

in two by her parents' continued fighting. Sophia's mother refused to come in to talk to me but I was able to work with the dad in developing a less hostile transition from his home to Sophia's mother's home. He began to stop arguing with Sophia's mother in front of Sophia. He worked out an arrangement with her mom in which he would call her Monday morning after Sophia had left for school to discuss any concerns about the weekend. Sophia's parents still had lots of things that they disagreed about but they did not do this in front of Sophia. Sophia's stomachaches diminished and she became more able to tell her dad on Sundays how much she missed him during the week.

Dropping off and picking up children is a very emotionally intense and important event. Both parents and children may be feeling a wide range of emotions. You may feel relieved that you are getting a break from sibling fighting and the stress of running your children to their various activities while simultaneously feeling sad and lonely about being separated from them. Your children may also be feeling a sense of loss over having to leave as well as excitement about being reunited with their other parent. Although the transition from one home to the other usually gets easier over time, all of you may continue to experience conflicting feelings each time your children shift from one home to the next. The following six tips will help make the transfer easier.

1. Prepare your children for the transfer by talking to them about how much you enjoyed being together. Let them know that they are going to have a good time with the other parent. This gives your children permission to enjoy that time. Assure them that you love them and will miss them. If you have a child who tends to worry about you while you are apart, let him or her know one of the things you will be doing while he or she is gone, such as painting the kitchen, having lunch with a friend, or finishing a book. This will help reduce the anxiety about leaving you.

2. Set up a phone time, the day of or before the transfer, to update the other parent about what has been happening to your children and to notify him or her of upcoming events. For example, "Spencer missed two days of school this week because he has an ear infection. He is taking one teaspoon of Amoxicillyn three

times a day," or, "Jose broke up with his girlfriend last night. He's pretty upset about it," or, "Tory has a swim meet Saturday at 8:00 A.M." This call should be made when the children are not listening. During this call try to stay focused on the children.

3. Have your children fed, bathed, and dressed, and return them from overnight parenting time with clean clothes.

4. Spend some time going over homework with your children before returning them to the other parent.

5. When dropping off your children, do not use the time as an opportunity to relay information or bring up concerns to the other parent. Just say something simple and positive such as, "Have a good time." Other matters can be relayed during your phone call. If you have crucial information to give the other parent, hand him or her a note about it. Do not give the note to your children. If you have difficulty seeing or talking to the other parent at all (especially common during the first several weeks after the initial separation), say good-bye to your children when the other parent is not present—before the children leave your house or your car.

6. The day before the transfer, be aware of changes that will affect your children physically. For example, if the other parent wakes the children up at 6:00 A.M. to take them to daycare, make sure you get them to bed early the night before. If you know that they'll be up late the night of the transfer, consider having them take a nap that afternoon. If you are having trouble doing this because of your feelings toward the other parent, keep in mind that you are doing this for your children's benefit and not to make the other parent's life easier. "One of the things that drove me crazy about my ex was that she was a health-food nut. She never let the kids have any sugar. Our parenting schedule was set up so that I would drop the kids off at school Monday mornings and she would pick them up after school. Every Monday she would yell at the kids for being hyper because of all the 'crap' I put in their lunches. I didn't think a few cookies made them

hyper but I couldn't convince her of that. My kids were upset about her yelling so I started putting healthier snacks in their lunches on Mondays. I still let them have cookies and candy the other days that they were with me but if I put the healthy stuff in on Mondays they don't have to get yelled at because of something I did" (Dominick, father of three).

Jot down in your Personal Notes section at the back of the book anything else you can think of that will make the transition from one home to another easier.

What to Do During Your Parenting Time

"I knew my dad didn't really want to be with me. When we got to his house he'd go work on his computer and leave me alone. During dinner he'd read the paper and then take me back to Mom's. I think the only reason he demanded visitation was to get back at Mom" (Anthony, fourteen). Children feel rejected, as if the parents are just going through the motions, when parents do not spend time with them. Try, as much as possible, to schedule time with your adult friends and business trips when your children are with the other parent. Giving your children your time and attention tells them that you love and choose to be with them.

Do not try to compensate for lost time by buying too many gifts or giving into their every demand. Children need to know that parents are in control and that there are limits. They need to know that love is not for sale. Being at the center of a competition between their parents teaches your children to get their needs met through manipulation rather than by developing healthy problem-solving skills.

The following exercise will help you think of ways to spend quality time with your children during your parenting time.

EXERCISE 2: WHAT I LIKE TO DO WITH MY MOM/DAD

Step 1: Ask your child to circle the items below that he or she likes to do with you. If you have more than one child, use separate lists or have each child circle, in separate colors, what they like to do with you. You can then do these activities alone with each of your children or together as a family. If you do the activity with your children together, have each child take turns choosing what you will do. If there are any activities that you strongly dislike doing, eliminate them from the list. It will not be fun for you or your children if you are miserable the whole time you are engaged in the activity.

sit together on the couch and cuddle

read a story

ride bikes

make up stories

swim

put on a play or puppet show

roller blade

play board games

walk

play on the computer

sled

fly a kite

skate

go on a picnic

build a snowman or make snow angels and decorate them with birdseed

take a trip to the park

build a fort in the woods, snow, or house

play cards

sing songs together

have tea parties

go to the beach

go for car rides

hike in the woods

fish

play catch

play soccer

shoot baskets

build a model

take piggyback rides

draw

collect rocks, shells, or leaves

dance

eat breakfast foods for dinner

play Simon Says

bake

tell jokes

thumb wrestle

plant something

do a craft or wood-working project

use shampoo lather to make fancy hairdos

lay on the grass, look up at the sky, and decide what the shapes of the clouds resemble

Step 2: With your child, list other activities you enjoy doing together in the Personal Notes section at the back of this book. Think of activities that don't cost a lot of money. The purpose of the activity is not to entertain your children but to be with them.

Step 3: Do one of the activities right now. This will communicate that you will follow through and spend time with the child in the ways that he or she has suggested. Saying "later" when you have promised to do something with your children creates distrust and anger. Your children need to believe that you will keep your promises and trust that they can still count on you to be there for them.

Step 4: Pick another activity and write on the calendar when you will do it.

When I am having difficulty finding things to do with my children, I use the book *365 TV-Free Activities* by Steve and Ruth Bennett to help me think of something fun to do. I have my children pick an activity from the book and we read and do it together. This and other such books are listed in the reference section at the back of this book. The Internet is another source of creative ideas. My daughter and I learned how to make rain coats out of Ziploc bags for her Beanie Babies on the Internet. The book *101 Ways to Make Your Child Feel Special* by Vicki Lansky also has many fun activities. I modified one of her ideas for the following exercise.

EXERCISE 3: COAT OF ARMS ACTIVITY

Materials
construction paper
crayons or markers
clear contact or shelving paper
pencils

Step 1: Sit down with all of your children and let them know you are going to create a coat of arms to represent your family. Explain that a coat of arms is a symbol of your family. If you have older children, you may want to show them pictures from an encyclopedia that shows a coat of arms used in battle. Talk to them about how families during the Middle Ages put symbols on the shields of armor to represent their clan or family.

Step 2: Talk to your children about interests that you all have in common. This could be sports, reading, music, camping, and so on.

Step 3: Choose a symbol that you or your children can draw that represents this activity. For example, if you all enjoy music, you could pick a quarter note to be your symbol. If you like to camp, a tent could be your symbol.

Step 4: Draw an outline of a coat of arms.

Step 5: Draw the symbol inside the coat of arms.

Step 6: Color it.

Step 7: Cover the paper with clear contact paper.

Step 8: Cut it out.

Step 9: Hang it on your door.

It is normal for your children to miss you when they are with the other parent and miss the other parent when they are with you. Allow your children to call the other parent when they are with you. This is especially true for younger children who need more frequent contact with both parents. It is also particularly important if you live more than two hours away from the other parent and it has been over a week since your children have seen him or her. If talking directly to the parent is not feasible, encourage your children to write down or make a tape of things they wish to communicate. When you're not with your children, send them brief notes and cards letting them know you are thinking about them. In the Personal Notes section at the back of this book, jot down some ideas for communicating with your children when they are with their other parent. For example, if you and your children both have access to the Internet, send e-mail messages to each other.

Holidays

Holidays are a mixed blessing for divorced families. They can be very joyful, but also very stressful and painful. As we reminisce about past holidays and look through family albums we can't help but think about how it "used to be." In addition, many of us already feel inadequate as a result of too little time and money to fulfill our expectations. Divorce confounds this by requiring parents to split the time they have with their children. Do not try to make up for lost time or compete for your children's love and loyalty. Discuss with the other parent where and when your children will spend the holidays. For example, some parents have the children spend Christmas Eve with one parent and Christmas Day with the other. Others, particularly if the parents live a great distance from one another, try to avoid the stress created by rushing to different houses by rotating holidays. If your children are feeling sad about not being with the other parent, assure them that they will be experiencing two celebrations, one with each parent. Discuss your children's gift list with your former partner and decide together who will buy what. Keep in mind that the most valuable gift you can give your children is permission to love both parents.

Family Pets

"When I decided to leave my husband Jeremy, I didn't even think about what we would do about our dog Striker. I was so worried about the kids and how all of us were going to adjust to apartment living, I forgot to ask about the apartment's policy on pets. The kids were devastated when I told them Striker couldn't come with us, that he would have to stay with Dad. My son Joey told me that if Striker wasn't going, neither was he. My daughter Melissa started yelling about how I always hated Striker messing up the house and that she hoped I was happy now that I'd found a way to get rid of him" (Cynthia, mother of two).

When you are making your decisions about parenting time, consider what to do with the family pets. Using the tips for a successful meeting in chapter 5, sit down with your children and the other parent and explore your options. Talk to your children about the needs of their pets as well as their own feelings. Discuss the pros and cons of each option and then decide together what is in the best interests of the pet as well as each family member. This may take several family meetings as you may need to have each family member get more information on each option before making a final decision. For example, if one option is to give the dog to a Seeing Eye program, someone will need to find out if your dog qualifies.

"Both of my parents died when I was six. Fortunately, my grandmother was smart enough to realize that I needed my dog Buffy more than ever. My older sister told me later that she heard Grandma tell Grandpa, 'Buffy comes with the girls.' I clung to that dog throughout my childhood. He listened to me cry and licked my face to cheer me up. I don't know how I would have made it without him" (Helen, now twenty). Your children have suffered a major loss during the divorce and may use their pet to cling to, to have someone to talk to, and to help them feel that they are loved unconditionally. They will probably want their pet to travel back and forth between the two homes with them. If you are considering this, your family needs to answer the following questions before making a decision.

- Is the pet bonded to one particular family member? Some breeds, such as chows, tend to bond with one person. If this person is the parent, the pet may have difficulty tolerating the transition.

- Is the pet an outside pet? If the answer is yes, do both residents have a safe place outside for the pet?

- Does the pet travel well in the car?

- Are both parents willing to have this pet in their home?

- Who will be responsible to feed, walk, and bathe the pet?

- Who will be responsible for the cost of food, grooming, and vet services?

Animals, like children, need a set routine. If you do decide to have the pet travel with the child make sure that:

- The food and water dish or litter box are placed in the same spot each time the pet is in your home.

- The other parent knows if the pet is taking any medication.

- Both parents agree on who will be responsible for vet appointments, vaccination records, and so on.

Each year while we are on vacation, my daughter will say, "Jasmine misses me." This probably signifies that my daughter is really talking about her own feelings rather than the cat's. If your children have to leave their pet when they spend time with the other parent, they suffer a loss each time they have to leave their pet behind. It may help your children and the pet for the children to leave a shirt that they have worn in the animal's bed. This will help your children feel that they are doing something to comfort their pet and confirm that their pet still loves and needs them.

If neither parent is able to keep the family pet, decide together where the pet will go. Use the following questions to facilitate discussion.

- If the option is to give the pet to a friend of the family or relative, is this person willing to send photos or letters about the pet?

- Is it feasible and will it be emotionally better or worse for your children to visit the pet?

- If one option is to take the pet to the pound, what is the pound's policy regarding finding another home for the pet, putting the pet to sleep, or selling the pet to a research lab?

Although it may be difficult, involving your children in the decision making will aid in their acceptance of the final decision and help them cope with the change.

Long-Distance Parenting

If you and your children live in different states, the guidelines below will assist you in maintaining a relationship with them.

- Make sure that you visit each other's hometowns, rather than them or you visiting one town exclusively. One father who lived in the South wanted to reduce his children's stress at having to travel long distances to be with him, so he would travel to the northern state where his children lived with their mother and stay at a local hotel. His children would stay with him at the hotel for the weekend, and they had a great time swimming in the hotel pool together. During the summer, his children would then live with him in his home in the South. Another father had regular business near the town where his children lived. He would call their mother ahead of time and arrange to spend time with them whenever he was going to be in town. In addition his children would travel to live with him six weeks every summer and alternate school holidays.

- Establish a phone schedule in which you call your children weekly.

- Give your children self-addressed stamped envelopes so they can send you letters, pictures, report cards, and so on.

- Send your children and have them send you videos, photos, or audiocassettes of each other.

- If you both have access, send your children E-mail messages.

- Arrange for visits with relatives.

When a Parent Doesn't Visit

It is very difficult for children to understand why a parent would choose not to see them. Children often blame themselves and wonder what they did to alienate the parent. Their self-esteem often suffers and they feel unloved and abandoned. If the other parent chooses to not have any contact with your children, explain to them that this is not their fault. Help them accept that this parent is not capable of being the parent that they need and assist them in not blaming themselves. Assure them that it is not because they are not good enough, unlovable, or bad. If you don't know for sure why the other parent doesn't visit, tell your children that you don't know exactly what it is that keeps the other parent from missing out on having a relationship with them. It may help to suggest that some parents have serious problems that prevent them from spending time with their children. Explain that the other parent may feel too guilty or unhappy to visit. If you know that the other parent has a drug or alcohol addiction, talk to them about how the disease of addiction may prevent him or her from being a good parent. Assure them that you love them and point out that other adults love them. Encourage your children to spend time with other adults they like and trust. Let them know that being with family and friends who care about, appreciate, and love them will help them feel less lonely. Help teenagers and young adults understand that, despite their parent's behavior, they are capable of one day being good parents themselves, and point out the strengths they have that will make them good parents. If you sense that your children are having difficulty coping with not seeing the other parent, consider taking them to see a counselor or therapist. (Chapter 13 will assist you.)

Lack of Visitation Due to Inappropriate Behavior

If a parent is physically, sexually, or emotionally abusive, or otherwise unable to provide safe, proper care or supervision for your children, coparenting may not be possible. If you suspect that the other parent is abusive or has an emotional or mental condition that interferes with his or her ability to be a good parent, consult with a professional child therapist and an attorney to decide the most appropriate approach to custody and parenting time.

3

Parenting Rules

*"If there is anything that we wish to change in
the child, we should first examine it and see whether
it is not something that could be changed in
ourselves."*

—Carl Gustav Jung

KEY POINTS

- Do not undermine the other parent's authority by criticizing his or her rules in front of your children.
- Accept the fact that you cannot control what rules the other parent makes.
- Establish and enforce clear, reasonable, and enforceable rules in your home.

Your children need consistent limit setting and rules in both homes because these things give your children a sense of stability and teach them responsibility. And yes, it is okay for parents to have different rules.

"I hated it when Leroy let the kids eat in the living room, with the TV on. We had always eaten dinner as a family at the table. But I knew I couldn't control what Leroy did at his house. So, when the kids said, 'Dad lets us eat in front of the TV,' I just told them what my rule was. Once they figured out that I wasn't going to change my mind, they stopped arguing about it" (Tamika, mother of three teenagers). You and your former partner may have different rules. Do not undermine the other parent's authority by disagreeing or telling your children that the other parent is wrong. This will only encourage your children to learn to manipulate and resist authority. If the other parent has different rules, explain your rules and consistently enforce your rules in your home. Tell your children that it is okay to have different rules because people are different (not better or worse). If your children disagree with some of the rules, encourage them to discuss the matter with the parent who enforces them. This will teach your children direct communication skills. If there is a rule that you strongly disagree with, ask yourself, "Will this rule psychologically or physically damage my child?" and, "Is this rule unsafe?" If the answer to both is no, work on accepting the rule. You may think it is unreasonable that the other parent won't let your children have friends sleep over or stay up past 8:00 P.M. on the weekends but it won't scar them for life. Talk to the other parent about rules you disagree with when your children are not present. *It is important that you accept that you cannot change or control the other parent.* Support your children's adjustment in having to abide by two sets of rules. Encourage them to accept both parents' authority.

Make a list of the rules in your house. Most parents make too many rules and don't enforce them. The key is to make a few rules that are consistently enforced. You may want to give the other parent a copy of your rules—not to seek permission but to let him or her know what your expectations are. Ask the other parent what his or her rules are. This may even inspire him or her to make a list as well.

How to Write Clear, Reasonable, and Enforceable Rules

Write rules as statements, not questions. If you say to your child, "Will you empty the trash?" it appears that he has the option to say no. When you say, "Please empty the trash before you leave for school today," what you expect is clear. To make your rules effective, clarify your rules, choose reasonable rules, and write rules that you can enforce.

1. Clarify rules.

Household rules need to be clearly understood by both you and your children. Ask yourself, "If the boy next door read this rule, would he know if it has been followed?" For example, my definition of a clean room is that there are no toys on the floor, the bed is made, and clothes are hung up or put in drawers. My son's definition of a clean room is that everything is shoved in the closet or under the bed. My rule about cleaning his room, therefore, has to specify that there are no toys on the floor, the bed is made, and clothes are hung up or put in drawers. If your rule is well written, your child will know right away if he has broken it. He may argue that it is not fair or ask you why his sister doesn't have to do it, but he won't be able to honestly say that it was done. If the rule is that the garbage has to be emptied before 5:00 P.M. on Thursdays and at that time the cans have trash in them, it's clear that he has broken the rule. Parents should expect no more than the rule states; they can change or modify the rules later if they prove to be too vague.

2. Choose reasonable rules.

Make sure your child is capable of performing the rule. In addition, make sure that the time required to do it takes into account time needed for schoolwork, activities, rest, and family. Breaking tasks down into smaller steps and demonstrating tasks helps younger children understand what you want. For example, "Please empty all of the wastebaskets into a garbage bag, tie the bag up, and put the bag out by the curb, on the lawn, next to the driveway."

3. Choose rules that are enforceable.

Effective rules are ones you can enforce and directly observe. If you work until 5:00, telling your children they can't watch TV after school isn't a rule that you can enforce. I remember asking my brother one afternoon why he had a box of telephones in his trunk. He told me that he had made a rule that his teenage stepdaughter could talk on the phone during the week if she stuck to her curfew and got home by 11:00 on Friday and Saturday nights. She broke the rule, and because my brother had to work during the week and was not home to monitor phone use, he took the phones to work with him. Although this sounds extreme, it was the only way he could think of to enforce the rule.

EXERCISE 4: ARE MY RULES CLEAR, REASONABLE, AND ENFORCEABLE?

For each pair of rules below, circle the rule that is clear.

1. *Be nice to your sister.*

2. *Do not hit, poke, slap, or bite your sister.*

1. *Don't watch too much TV.*

2. *You may watch only two hours of TV a week. Let's sit down together on Sundays and decide which shows you would like to watch for the week.*

For each pair of rules below, circle the rule that is reasonable.

For your five-year-old daughter:

1. *Put the crystal glasses away.*

2. *Before you eat your breakfast, empty the cat's water dish in the sink and refill it with fresh water.*

For your eight-year-old son:

1. *Fill the lawn mower up with gas and mow the lawn.*

2. *Pick up the sticks in the front yard before you go to Jimmy's house.*

For each pair of rules below, circle the rule that is enforceable.

1. *Don't call your sister names on the way to school.*

2. *No calling names at the dinner table. If you call a name at the dinner table, you will have to leave the table and sit on the steps for five minutes.*

1. *Do your chores while I'm at work.*

2. *I will serve dinner each night after you set the table.*

The correct answer to all of the above rules is 2.

Whenever you make up a new rule, children will frequently break it. This is their way of testing out a change in their environment. I often warn parents that when they make a change in their parenting, their children's behavior usually gets worse before it gets better. Ignore behavior such as temper tantrums, whining, complaining, and pouting. When your child breaks the rule, say to them, "What is the rule?" If he or she doesn't respond, recite the rule in a neutral tone of voice and enforce it. Don't nag or yell, simply restate the rule. For example, if the rule is no TV in the morning until after breakfast and your child turns on the TV before breakfast, ask your child what the rule is. Restate the rule and turn off the TV. If your child complains but turns off the TV and starts eating breakfast, you should ignore the complaint and sit and eat breakfast with your child.

The following exercise will help you learn to consistently set up and enforce family rules.

EXERCISE 5: OUR RULES

Step 1: Start by creating and enforcing one family rule. Think of something that you want your child to do every day, and write it in the space below.

Step 2: Ask yourself:

Does the rule have a specific time limit?

Can you directly observe whether or not the rule is followed?

Does your child know how to do the task?

Step 3: Check for loopholes. Have a friend read the rule to see if it is clear.

Step 4: Tell your child the rule. Ask your child if he or she understands the rule and have him or her restate it.

Step 5: Post the rule where your child can see it, in the room where you enforce it. For example, if the rule is that your child needs to read for one hour before he or she can play Nintendo, post the rule above the Nintendo set.

Step 6: For one to two weeks focus on enforcing this rule.

Step 7: After you have mastered and consistently followed this rule, create another rule and follow steps 1–6.

Step 8: When you have practiced writing and enforcing two rules, write a few more, following steps 1–3. Do not add more rules than you can enforce.

Step 9: Post all of the rules in a central location on a sheet labeled "Family rules."

Step 10: Anytime you change, add, or eliminate a rule, post a revised version.

Establishing and maintaining rules will assist you in providing the structure and consistency that your children need during this time of immense change for all of you. Doing so will help you feel more in control and less like Erma Bombeck when she said, "When my kids become wild and unruly, I use a nice, safe playpen. When they're finished, I climb out."

4

Coparenting

KEY POINTS

- Develop mutual respect for your children's other parent.
- Encourage the relationship between your children and their other parent.
- Create a school folder that travels with your children between visits.
- Attend school and sporting events even if your former partner will be there.
- Do not discuss child support with or in front of your children.
- Use divorce mediation to settle disputes over custody and parenting time that you cannot settle together.

Imagine waking up in the middle of the night to the sound of your smoke alarm blaring. Your first instinct would be to run to your children's room, scoop them up, and carry them to safety. You would probably walk through smoke and fire, or any crisis, risking your own life to save your children. Divorce is a crisis for your children. They need you to work together with the other parent to help them through this crisis. Your marriage may not have survived the fire but your relationship with the other parent will continue as long as your children are alive. Whether you spend one day a month or every day with your children, you and your former partner continue to be coparents. Coparenting involves cooperatively working with your children's other parent in an effort to assist your children in developing into socially and emotionally healthy adults. It involves communicating with one another concerning the needs of the children. Cooperative coparenting means considering your children's need to love both parents instead of focusing on your feelings toward the other parent. You do this because you understand that your children's need to see the other parent is more important than your need to punish him or her. Healthy coparenting is a way to carry your children through the crisis of divorce to safety.

Picture your child on her wedding or graduation day as she looks out at the family and friends who have gathered to witness the event. Will she be focusing on how happy she feels or will she be worrying about whether her parents are going to fight? Throughout the rest of your life, you and your former partner will be parents and grandparents and maybe even great-grandparents together. You can struggle and fight your way through each developmental milestone in your children's lives or you can learn to celebrate them together. In the Personal Notes section at the back of this book, write down what kind of relationship between you and your former partner would be most beneficial for your children.

Developing Respect for the Other Parent

Developing mutual respect for your children's other parent will help make you effective coparents. Follow the golden rule of coparenting: Treat the other parent like you want to be treated. This is difficult if he or she doesn't treat *you* with respect, but keep in mind that you are doing this for your children's survival and not for the other parent's benefit. Do not snicker or sneer at something the other parent says or something your child relays to you. Do not attempt to convey to your children that you are the better parent. If you are worried that showing mutual respect will confuse your children into thinking that their parents will get back together, avoid talking to your children about your feelings toward the other parent. Focus instead on the other parent's positive qualities as a parent.

To help you develop respect for the other parent, turn to the Personal Notes section at the back of this book and write down three instances in which he or she did well in the parental role. (For example, showing up on time for parenting time, praising your daughter for a good score on a test, attending your son's concert, or agreeing to pay for half of the cost of school pictures.)

Supporting Your Children's Relationship With the Other Parent

"It was hard for me to hear Crystal tell Mark what a good daddy he was. I felt that if he was such a good dad he would have tried harder to make the marriage work. Despite how I felt, I didn't tell my daughter what a lousy father I thought he was for leaving us. I knew that she would adjust better to the divorce if I encouraged her to have a good relationship with him" (Sue, mother of a five-year-old girl). Support your children in loving and building a relationship with the other parent. Do not say to them, "If your father/mother really loved you . . ." Do not allow your feelings of being betrayed to interfere with your support of your children's need to love and be loved by your former partner. Just as you are able to love a new baby without loving your other children less, your children can love more than one parent. If your child phones you while he or she is with the other parent, do not ask, "Do you miss me?" or, "Do you want to come home?" As painful as it may be for you, remember that your children are home when they are with the other parent. They will develop healthier relationships if they don't have to choose between loving you and loving the other parent. The following exercise will help you communicate to your children that it is okay to love both parents.

EXERCISE 6: HOW DO WE LOVE YOU? LET US COUNT THE WAYS

Do this exercise with each of your children, preferably separately.

Materials

crayons, chalk, or markers

pencils, pens

drawing paper

Step 1: Gather the above supplies and sit down with your child at a table. Tell him or her that you are going to draw or write about how your love can be illustrated. Say, "I'd like you to draw a picture of how we show love for each other." If your child resists drawing, you can instead ask him or her to write down or just tell you how you show love for each other.

Step 2: After your child has drawn the picture, ask him or her to tell you about it.

Step 3: Ask your child to draw a picture of how he or she and the other parent show love for each other.

Step 4: Again, ask your child to tell you about the picture.

Step 5: Tell your child how much you enjoyed being together. Put the picture of you and your child on the refrigerator door or other prominent place. This communicates that you value their work. Ask your child if he or she would like to give the other parent the picture of them.

Encourage other family members to support your children in having a relationship with the other parent. Sometimes, in a divorce, extended family demands that the children remain loyal to one parent. They say hostile things about the other parent in front of the children. When my sister was going through her divorce, I made the mistake of, in a joking way, putting down my niece and nephew's father in front of them. I thought I was supporting my sister. Instead, I was hurting her children.

Your children also need to continue to have a relationship with both sets of grandparents, aunts, uncles, and cousins. Allow them to spend time with extended family and encourage them to phone and write letters. One grandmother, after her grandchildren moved out of state, made a mini-photo album of their time together each time her grandchildren came to visit. She kept one copy and mailed another copy to each of her grandchildren.

Do not criticize the other parent's family, friends, or new spouse. If you think family members are badmouthing you, speak directly to them about it. Demonstrate to your children, through your behavior, that negative things they say about you are not true. Your children have lost enough in the divorce. Support them in continuing to spend time with family who love them. In the Personal Notes section at the back of this book, make a list of names, addresses, and phone numbers of family and friends who love your children. Give your children a copy of this list and encourage them to call, write letters, or e-mail these people whenever they wish.

Communicating with Each Other About Important Issues

Major decisions should be made jointly. This includes major medical, dental, and psychological treatment; grade and special education placement; or change of schools. Both parents should have access to physicians, therapists, educators, law enforcement personnel, or other professionals that are involved with your children. Inform the other parent, in advance, of any scheduled meetings with these professionals.

Create a school folder that travels back and forth with each of your children between visits. The folder should include notes from teachers, homework, schoolwork, report cards, sport schedules, flyers about upcoming events, and information concerning school pictures, open houses, or parent-teacher conferences. Communicate to your children's teachers and school counselors that you have set up this system, and encourage them to place items directly in the folder. The cooperative effort between you, the other parent, and the school can enhance your children's academic achievement and emotional adjustment. Do not include any notes to the other parent from you. If your children are having problems at school, communicate this to the other parent by phone, through the mail, or in person. The following exercise will help you compose a letter to school and organize a school folder.

EXERCISE 7: CREATING A SCHOOL FOLDER

Step 1: Communicate with the other parent that you want to create a school folder that travels back and forth with each of your children, and that this folder will only be used to exchange items relating to school.

Step 2: Use the sample letter below for each child and give a copy to the other parent. Ask him or her for feedback.

Step 3: Tell each of your children that you are going to create a school folder together. Have them pick out and decorate a two-pocket folder.

Step 4: Label the left side Notes Going Home and the right side Notes to Teacher.

Step 5: Send the letter to each of your children's teachers.

Step 6: After a parent has reviewed a document in the folder, he or she should initial it.

Dear _____ (teacher's name),
     In an effort to facilitate communication between
_____ (child's full name), the school,
and _____'s (child's name) parents,
we would like to create a school folder that goes back and
forth each day with _____ (child's
name).
     Please encourage _____
(child's name) to place any notes, report cards, homework,
or flyers directly in the left side of the folder. This folder is
_____ (color of folder) and is labeled School
Folder. We will place any papers or notes that you would
like returned in the right pocket of the folder. Every other
week we will remove old papers from the folder that both
parents have initialed.

Please let us know if you have any suggestions for the folder and please feel free to call us if you have any questions. _____ (mother's name) can be reached during the day at _____ and in the evenings at _____. _____ (father's name) can be reached during the day at _____ and in the evenings at _____.

We will start sending this folder Monday, _____ (date to begin).

Education is a high priority in our family and we appreciate your help in supporting _____'s (child's name) academic achievement.

Sincerely,

_____ (father's name)

_____ (mother's name)

Parents, when possible, should consider helping out in the classroom. Sharing a skill you have with your children's class helps your children feel special and can facilitate communication between you and the school. For example, my children's father does chemistry experiments one day each year in each of our children's classrooms. My children take great pride in these demonstrations.

Both parents should go to school and sporting events. School open houses, concerts, plays, recitals, and sports allow children an opportunity to be the center of attention, which builds their self-esteem. Your children already feel different from children whose parents are still together. Bonita, fifteen, talks about how she felt when her mom refused to come to any school function if Bonita's father was going to be there. "When my teacher said, 'Make sure your parents come to the open house,' it was easy for the other kids. They just had to remember to tell their parents about it. I had to decide which parent to invite and what excuse I was going to make up to explain why the other parent wasn't there." Knowing that both parents will attend school functions will help your children feel more normal. Do not use these events to discuss problems with the other parent. It is humiliating for your children to see you argue in public. If avoiding an argument with the other parent is too difficult or if it is too painful to sit together, sit in another area of the auditorium or classroom. Remember that these events are celebrations of your children's achievements. Your children deserve the privilege of having both parents involved.

Jenny, eight, was hit by a car while riding her bike. Her dad called her mom right away and told her what hospital they were going to. "I almost didn't call Catherine (Jenny's mom) because I knew she would blame me for the accident. The look on Jenny's face when she saw her mom come into the emergency room, however, told me I had done the right thing by calling. Jenny was in a lot of pain and very scared. She needed both of us to hold her hand as the doctor put on the cast." Every parent is aware that accidents happen and crises occur. In an emergency, your children need both parents more than ever. They need you to put your energy into helping them heal rather than blaming the other parent for the injury or illness. If your children get hurt and need medical attention, call the other parent immediately. Tell the other parent about major events that occur while your children are with you. This information can assist the other parent in helping your children through life's tragedies.

Child Support

Child support is another important issue that requires open communication between the parents. Pay your child support! You may not want to give money to your former partner, but your children may feel unwanted when a parent doesn't pay child support. Of course, you should never discuss child support with your children. If you do not have enough money to buy them something, tell them you don't have it. You do not have to explain why. Use this opportunity to teach money management skills.

"Every time Dad was late sending the check, Mom wouldn't let us go see him. It was so unfair. Why should we be punished because she was mad at him?" (Pamela, twelve). Do not refuse to allow your children to see the other parent for this reason. Even though you may depend on this money, threatening to withhold parenting time hurts your children. It helps to remember that spending time with both parents is a basic need for your children rather than a privilege that the other parent must earn. Telling your children that they can't see the other parent until the child support is paid is like refusing to feed your daughter until her brother cleans his room. Your children cannot control their parents' actions. They have done nothing wrong and need to be with both parents.

If you are unsuccessful in talking to the other parent about overdue child support, consult with a family therapist, friend of the court worker, or an attorney. However, *be extremely cautious about taking the other parent to court.* Legal battles are often drawn out and emotionally and financially costly for parents and their children. "When my mom remarried, we moved onto David's farm. My dad was really mad because it meant I was going to go to a different school. He thought my going to some 'hick' school was going to hurt my chances of getting into college. He took my mom to court and got the judge to stop her from switching schools until the court date in December. For the first half of the year my mom had to drive me to my old school. The judge finally decided that the school near David's house was just as good as my old one so I had to switch schools in the middle of the year. What a pain! I think Dad was just jealous that Mom finally found someone she could be happy with" (Callia, fourteen). Legal battles between parents are usually emotionally damaging to your children. Clearly evaluate your reasons for initiating a court proceeding. Is it really your *only* option? People sometimes use these battles as a way of maintaining their severed relationship to avoid the pain and unhappiness that may come upon realizing that the relationship is permanently over. Accept that the marriage has ended and move on. If you drag the other parent through court, you will drag and possibly scar your children along with it. (Chapter 12 will help you learn to move on.)

Mediation is an alternative to litigation. Most states offer or mandate divorce mediation, which allows parents to resolve conflicts through the use of a neutral third party. The mediator guides the parents through the divorce process and helps them reach a mutually satisfactory agreement. The mediator then usually writes up a summary of this agreement for the parents to review with their attorney. Mediation is a good option for parents who are planning on coparenting for the following reasons.

- It facilitates compromise and cooperation rather than competition between parents.

- It gives the parents—who know their children best—rather than the judge the power to make decisions about their children.

- It helps avoid court battles that often have negative emotional consequences for you and your children.

- It saves time and money.

- It assists parents in making decisions based on what is in the children's best interest rather than on emotions.

- It helps clarify issues and reduce anger and bitterness.

The mediator can also help you work out a tentative parenting plan that will outline when your children will be with each parent. Try this plan out for a month or two before putting it in your settlement agreement. At the end of the trial period, discuss with the other parent any changes either of you feel are needed, and revise your plan. If your children have concerns about the parenting time schedule, let them know that you will listen and consider their thoughts and feelings. In your Personal Notes section at the back of this book, write down any questions you can think of that you would like to ask a mediator.

Mediation is not appropriate in cases in which one parent cannot effectively negotiate or in cases of emotional or physical spousal abuse. However, in most cases, mediation can assist parents in focusing on the needs of their children, address their concerns, and facilitate communication.

A final tip: At the mediation session, put a photograph of your children on the table. This will help you focus on their needs rather than on your feelings about the other parent.

5

Communicating More Effectively

KEY POINTS

- Use "I" messages to communicate things you'd like changed.
- Take time to think about what you'd like to say.
- Do not ask your children about the behavior of the other parent.
- Do not tell your children to keep secrets from the other parent.
- Talking about the divorce is not what is causing the pain.
- Spend time individually with each of your children.
- Listen to your children. Pay attention to what they are saying and feeling.
- Keep communication open.
- Encourage expression of feelings.
- Teach your children how to express feelings in a productive, positive manner.
- Provide stability by continuing to observe family traditions.

"I couldn't communicate with Bob when we were married—how do you expect me to do it when we're divorced?" (Helen, mother of four). It may seem impossible to communicate with your ex, but ending a conflict-ridden dysfunctional marriage and working on developing a new coparenting relationship with the other parent can result in better communication. You *can* learn to communicate with the other parent, even when that person is uncooperative. It is essential to your children's well being.

How to Use "I" Messages

Throughout the divorce, practice positive communication through the use of "I" messages. The goal of the "I" message is for the other parent to understand exactly what you want changed. "I" messages involve clearly speaking in the here and now, in a nonjudgmental tone of voice. "I" messages relay feelings and target a specific idea; they tell the other parent how you are feeling and what you see is the problem. They work because they focus on behavior rather than attacking someone, which helps the other person focus on what you want changed rather than having to defend him- or herself. "I" statements force you to take time to think about what you want to say rather than speaking the first thing that comes to you, which may be negative or sarcastic.

"I" messages have three parts: state how you feel, identify the problem, and state what you would like the person to do. The following examples should help make this clear.

State how you feel:

Direction for Effective Communication	Negative Communication	"I" Message
Begin your sentence with "I feel ..." instead of "You ..."	"You never bring Aaron back on time."	"I worry when you bring Aaron back late on Sundays."
Say how the person's behavior affected you.	"You didn't send Janelle's math book again. You're such a jerk."	"I cannot help Janelle do her homework when you don't send her math book with her on Fridays."
Take ownership of your feelings rather than blaming the other person.	"You make me so mad when you tell Sue to keep secrets from me."	"I feel angry when you tell Sue to keep secrets from me."
Using one or two words, tell the other person how their behavior affects you. State an emotion.	"Why didn't you tell me when Jacob is having trouble in school?"	"I feel frustrated when you don't tell me when Jacob is having trouble in school."

Identify the problem:

Direction for Effective Communication	Negative Communication	"I" Message
Describe the parent's behavior, not his or her character. Be specific.	"Why don't you ever bring Michael's hockey skates back? You are so inconsiderate."	"I feel frustrated when you don't bring Michael's hockey skates back with him. Please bring his skates when you return him from your parenting time."

Direction for Effective Communication	*Negative Communication*	*"I" Message*
Describe things in a factual manner rather than attacking or threatening the person.	"I'm not your maid anymore. Next time you send Sandy back with dirty clothes, I'm going to send her back with the same dirty clothes."	"I feel taken for granted when you send Sandy back with dirty clothes. Please wash her clothes before you return her on Sunday."
Avoid making assumptions about the other parent's motivations.	"You don't care about Simone."	"I felt sad for Simone when she cried about the canceled trip to the zoo that you promised her. Please don't make promises to her unless you are sure you can keep them."
Focus on what is currently happening that is affecting you and not on past mistakes. Bringing up the past will place the other parent's attention on defending himself or herself rather than on cooperation.	"Why can't you get here on time for a change? You missed Jill's concert last week, you were an hour late for Luke's recital, and now you come in the middle of Jenny's track meet. Why do you even bother showing up at all?"	"I feel irritated when you're late for our children's school and sporting events. I would like you to be on time for Jenny's track meet on Saturday."

Make a specific request for change:

Direction for Effective Communication	*Negative Communication*	*"I" Message*
State the request in positive terms.	"Don't forget to take George to get his allergy shot."	"Please take George to get his weekly allergy shot on Friday."

Be specific in your requests so that you both are clear about what you are requesting.	"Don't let Becky stay up late."	"Please put Becky to bed by eight o'clock."
Avoid using "always" and "never." When you use these words, the other parent's reaction is usually to defend him- or herself rather than focusing on the current problem.	"You never pick up Jessica on time."	"I feel irritated when you are late picking up Jessica. I would appreciate it if you would pick her up at six."
Be direct in your requests rather than hinting or presuming.	Please think about giving me a copy of Jamie's report card.	Please give me a copy of Jamie's report card.

Gene, mother of five, talked about how "I" messages helped her communicate with her former partner. "After the divorce, every time Jerry did something that bugged me, I blew up. We'd get into a shouting match and nothing would change. At a parenting class that I had taken at my church I learned to use 'I' messages, and I started using them when I talked to Jerry. Whenever he did something really stupid, I'd first call my friend Lisa. Lisa helped me put what I wanted to say into an 'I' message. I'd then call Jerry and explain how I was feeling and what I wanted changed. It took a lot of practice, but after a while I stopped needing to call Lisa first and found that Jerry and I were shouting at each other less and were actually able to focus on the kids."

Take time to think about what you will say. This will help you control the expression of your feelings. Initially, it may feel awkward using "I" messages, so use a friend to practice them with before trying them out. With practice, "I" messages will become a useful tool in communicating effectively not only with the other parent, but with your children, other family members, in-laws, colleagues at work, and friends.

EXERCISE 8: "I" MESSAGES

Below are several scenarios. Fill in the blanks to create an "I" message for each scenario.

1. Your children are brought back two hours late.

I feel _____ when you _____, and I would like you to _____.

2. Your children are taken to an R-rated movie.

I feel _____ when you _____, and I would like you to _____.

3. The other parent fails to give you the note from the teacher that asked you to have your child bring in supplies for a school project.

I feel _____ when you _____, and I would like you to _____.

4. Child support is two weeks late.

I feel _____ when you _____, and I would like you to _____.

5. Your children's stepmother takes your six-year-old daughter to the mall to get her ears pierced.

I feel _____ when you _____, and I would like you to _____.

6. The other parent yells at you in front of your children.

I feel _____ when you _____, and I would like you to _____.

7. Now write your own problem situation and an "I" message to respond to it.
   Problem:

_____

_____

_____

I feel _____ when you _____, and I would like you to _____.

If the other parent responds to your attempts to use "I" messages by saying he or she doesn't care about how you feel, respond with a nondefensive statement and repeat what you would like changed. "I understand that. Please have Susan ready on time," or, "I can hear it in your voice. Please send next week's check on time." If the conversation heats up and either of you start yelling, disengage and set up another time to talk. Taking a time-out will give both of you a chance to cool down and think about what you want to communicate.

If you meet with continued resistance, ask questions. "I need to know how Kenny is doing in school. How do you suggest I get this information?" "How do you think we can work out a solution to this problem?" "What do you see as the solution to this?"

Steven Covey, in *The 7 Habits of Highly Effective People*, said if he had to choose the single most important thing in interpersonal communication it would be to "seek first to understand, then to be understood." Working on improving your listening skills will help you facilitate the communication between you and the other parent. In your Personal Notes section at the back of this book, jot down any ideas you can think of to keep communication with the other parent open.

Keep the Kids Out of the Middle

"I hated it when Dad would ask me about Mom's new boyfriend. It made me feel like I was being a spy" (Tyrone, eleven). Do not ask your children about the behavior of the other parent. Asking them about what the other parent is doing places your children in a no-win situation. Children feel disloyal when they reveal information about the other parent. If they want to remain loyal to the other parent, it gives them two options: they can tell you that it's none of your business, or they can lie to you. This makes them very uncomfortable because they know that neither option is acceptable. If they tell you what the other parent did, they risk upsetting the other parent and risk upsetting you, if they anticipate that you won't like the information. Asking your children about what the other parent is doing also gives them power to manipulate you by revealing significant information or withholding information about the other parent.

Equally important is to avoid telling your children to keep secrets from the other parent. If you are doing something that you don't want the other parent to find out about, don't do it when your children are present. Having to keep secrets increases children's anxiety and interferes with their ability to trust. Your children need to have an open and honest relationship with both parents. Rather than spending your time with your children talking about the other parent, spend it on building your relationship with them.

Keep Communication with Your Children Open

Maria, a divorced mother of two girls, talked about one daughter's reaction to the divorce. "Angie was angry all the time. She kept telling me how much she hated me and that I drove her dad away. It was so hard to listen to her yelling all the time even though I knew she needed to get it out." The time period immediately after telling your children about the divorce will be emotionally intense. Children and parents will be dealing with their feelings of loss, anger, and guilt. It can be very painful for parents to see their children hurt, watch them cry, and listen to the anger they express. Your children, however, need to grieve. Grief is normal, natural, and healthy. (See chapter 6 for further discussion on the stages of grief.) Remember that talking about the divorce is not what is causing the pain. It is the loss from the divorce and the subsequent changes that children worry about that creates the pain. Talking about the divorce can give children strength to handle difficult situations and provide them with a supportive environment in which to deal with the overwhelming and diverse feelings that they may experience.

Sara talked about her struggle to get her seventeen-year-old daughter to talk about the divorce. "For the first few months after Ken moved out Monica wouldn't talk to me. Whenever I brought up the subject she would run to her room and slam the door. If I tried to go into her room she'd shout at me to leave her alone. I kept telling her I loved her, it was okay for her to be angry, and I was here for her if she wanted to talk. I didn't give up, despite how exhausted and frustrated I felt. One night I heard her crying in her room. I knocked on the door and asked her what was wrong. She said Kyle (her boyfriend) had broken their date again. She asked me what she was doing wrong. She talked about how hurt and angry she was and how she thought he was seeing someone else. I sat on her bed, handing her Kleenex and listening for the rest of the night. After that, things got easier and she was able to talk about the divorce too. She told me that she thought I drove her dad away and how much she hated my working. Things aren't perfect and we still argue about her curfew and homework, but we are closer now than we were before and I'm proud of how well she's handling the divorce."

Allow time, later on, to talk about the divorce even if your children are resistant to the topic when you first tell them. If they run to their rooms crying, let them know that you love them and you are available to talk when they are ready. Although it may be difficult to talk to your children about the divorce, keeping communication open is vital to their recovery, so provide relaxed, safe opportunities for discussion. For example, take walks, go for rides in the car, sit together on a park bench, or go out to lunch. The next time you're in a traffic jam, turn off the radio and use the opportunity to open a discussion. While you're waiting an hour for your daughter's dance class, ask your son what is happening in his life. Children may have difficulty talking about their feelings, so if they say they don't want to talk, don't pressure them. Let them know that you love them and that when they are ready you will listen. Remember, children often want to talk at times that are not convenient for you, such as when you're fixing dinner, reading the paper, or about to leave the house to go to work. As much as possible, take advantage of these opportunities. Dinner and the paper can wait an hour. Your children may not, in an hour, be willing to talk and may interpret your putting them off as further rejection. This is a very sensitive time for your children. They need you to show them that they are important and loved. If you cannot talk at the moment your child wants to, give a specific time that you will talk to him or her and follow through on giving your child this time. Do not postpone it again.

Spend Time Individually with Each of Your Children

Meeting with your kids separately, on an ongoing basis, will provide opportunities for them to voice their individual concerns. Parents with hectic lives often end up doing what is immediate rather than what is important. When you plan your week, consider what is truly important to you and schedule time to talk to your children. As with physical exercise, if you schedule time for it daily you will be much more likely to actually do it rather than feel guilty about never finding the time for it. Use the following exercise to help you plan time to spend with your children.

EXERCISE 9: COMMUNICATION OPPORTUNITY LIST

Complete for each of your children. Ask your child for input.

Child's name: _____

_____ (child's name) favorite place:

_____

_____

_____ (child's name) favorite thing to do with me:

_____

_____

Times and places to talk: _____

_____

Another way of encouraging your children to talk about the divorce is by asking them about friends of theirs whose parents are divorced. This will help you clear up any misunderstandings that they may have about divorce and remind them that they are not alone.

You will have difficulty helping your children cope with their feelings if you don't know how they are feeling. Treat each child's comments and questions as important regardless of his or her age. Answer your children's questions honestly but avoid lengthy explanations and unnecessary details. For example, you do not need to tell your children that the other parent has been sleeping with the next-door neighbor. Such details may make it difficult for you at this point to avoid putting down the other parent, but keep in mind that you are doing this for your children and not for the protection of the other parent.

Assure your children that they can continue to talk about how the divorce is affecting them. Because they may not feel comfortable asking the questions out loud, tell them that they can write down any questions. After you have talked to the children together, set up a time to talk to each of them separately. Older children may avoid asking questions or expressing their true feelings in front of younger siblings, partly to protect their younger brothers and sisters and partly to avoid looking stupid. Talking to your children separately will provide opportunities for your children to express individual concerns and will communicate to them that their feelings and concerns are important to you. Continue to let your children know how the divorce will affect them. If one parent will be returning to work or if the kids will have to change schools, give them opportunities to talk about how they feel and how they can better cope with these changes.

Listen to Your Children

"The first duty of love is to listen."
—Paul Tillich

One of the mistakes I make as a parent is that I tend to talk too much. Learn to be more comfortable with periods of silence. Children will often say something to fill the silence if you just sit back and wait. During the family meeting and throughout the divorce, pay attention to what your children are saying. What are the feelings underneath what they say? Are they feeling angry, sad, abandoned, frightened, or relieved? Acknowledge your children's right to have these feelings and to let others know how they feel. Your children need for you to give them permission to talk about the divorce, because they may be afraid that they'll hurt you by talking about it. If you don't let them know that it is all right to talk about the divorce, they may try to cover up or deny their feelings, which will interfere with their recovery. Let your children cry. Hold them or hug them. If they ask to be left alone, let them know that you love them and acknowledge their feelings. They will be more open to talking about the divorce as you become a better listener. The following ten steps will help improve your listening skills and communicate to your children that what they say is important.

Ten Steps to Becoming a Better Listener

1. Provide an opening for discussion by saying, "Tell me what you've been thinking," or, "It may help to talk about it?"

2. Acknowledge that you are listening by saying, "I see," "uh-uh," "mm-hmm," or "okay."

3. Remain silent but nod your head as you allow your children to talk.

4. Restate what you think your child said and ask him/her if that is what he/she is saying.

5. Look at your children when they are talking to you.

6. Stand or sit near your children when they are talking.

7. Touch them on the arm or shoulder.

8. Don't interrupt them when they are talking.

9. Avoid invalidating what they are saying with comments like, "You shouldn't feel that way."

10. Don't give advice.

The STEP (Systematic Training for Effective Parenting) program teaches parents to remember the acronym SOFTEN, which stands for Smile, Open body language, Forward lean, Touch and Tone of voice, Eye contact, and Nod. Your facial expression, tone of voice, and actions all communicate your willingness to listen to your children's feelings. In your Personal Notes section at the back of this book, write down what you hear your children telling you about how the divorce is affecting them.

When Frank and Beth told their six-year-old son Jeremy about the divorce, he moved to the end of the couch, put his fingers in his ears, and started humming. When Beth tried to hug him, he pushed her hand away and stared at the floor. Frank and Beth waited until Jeremy stopped humming, and told him that they loved him and that they understood that he was angry.

Rejecting your affection at this time may be a way for your children to express their anger. Tell your children it is all right for them to be angry and that you still love them. Continue to listen to what they are saying as well as what they are avoiding talking about.

During the family meeting and throughout the divorce, use reflective listening to aid you in communicating with your children. Reflective listening, which involves letting your children know that you recognize and accept how they are feeling, helps you focus on and understand your children's feelings. Colleen's eight-year-old daughter April said to her, "If you loved us, you would come back home." Colleen responded to April with, "I understand that you miss me and that you're angry about the divorce." This "open" communication told April that her mom heard the feelings behind her words and it was okay for April to talk about how she felt. Starting a sentence with phrases like "it seems," "it appears," "you sound," or "I can see why you were" will help communicate that you aren't assuming you always know what your children are feeling. Rather, open responses tell your children that you are trying to *understand* how they're feeling. Open communication encourages your children to talk. It communicates that you understand and want to hear what they have to say. Closed communication such as moralizing, preaching, and judging tends to discourage your children from sharing their feelings with you. The following chart will help you distinguish between open and closed communication.

Child's Statement	Closed Parent Communication	Open Parent Communication
"My stomach hurts. I'm sick. Call Daddy."	"Get out of bed. You're okay. You'll be late for school."	"I know you miss your daddy and you wish he was here. How about if we call him after school today?"
"Macaroni and cheese again! Can't you cook anything else?"	"You should be grateful you have food on your plate. I work darn hard all day. If you don't like it, why don't you go eat at Dad's?"	"I understand it's been hard for you to adjust to us not having as much money and eating out less often. How about if we plan some meals that you like but are still within our budget?"
"You're a liar, you said we would always be a family!"	"Don't talk to me that way!"	"You seem really angry and hurt that Dad and I won't be together anymore."

If these statements from your children sound disrespectful, keep in mind that the purpose of open communication is to help your children talk about their feelings. Teaching respect is a valuable lesson that children need to learn and it is okay to place limits on swearing and calling you names. Keep in mind, however, that focusing primarily on teaching respect at this time may distract you from keeping communication open. Remember that your goal is to help your children understand that the divorce is not their fault, you love them, you will listen to what they have to say, and you understand and accept their feelings. How to help your children express their feelings in an appropriate manner is discussed later on in this chapter.

EXERCISE 10: OPEN COMMUNICATION

Step 1: For each comment below, write an example of an open communication response.

Child's statement:
"You never loved Mom and you don't love me."

Open parent response:

_____

_____

_____

Child's statement:
"You never let me do anything fun. If Mom were still here, she would let me go."

Open parent response:

_____

_____

_____

Child's statement:
"Even Dad's girlfriend thinks you're a witch. I'm calling Dad."

Open parent response:

_____

_____

_____

Child's statement:
"I hate you. I don't want to be divorced."

Open parent response:

_____

_____

_____

Step 2: Read each of your open responses out loud and answer the questions below to check if they are open communications.

1. Does your remark state what your child feels?

2. Did you avoid being critical, sarcastic, and negative?

3. Does it sound as if you're trying to understand your children's feelings, or telling them how they should feel?

Step 3: Write a negative comment that one of your children has made and develop an open communication that you could use to respond.

Child's statement:

_____

_____

_____

Open parent response:

_____

_____

_____

Step 4: Repeat Step 2 for the response you just wrote.

Ask Your Children to List Questions and Concerns About the Divorce

Encourage your children to identify and write a list of all the issues they want to discuss. Have each child write down any questions, worries, fears, or concerns they have about the divorce. If they resist writing, ask them to tell you their concerns and write them down for them. If they enjoy working on the computer, put the form on the computer and have them fill it in.

Leigha's father asked her to list the things about the divorce that she wanted to talk about. Leigha, nine, said she was fine about the divorce and didn't need to talk about it. She then began talking about her cat that had run away last year and her dog that was hit by a car. Her father talked with her about her feelings and what she had done to feel better when Slippers hadn't come home and Brandy had died. When children and adults suffer a loss, thoughts and feelings from other losses often arise. Your children may identify previous losses (such as the death of a pet or family member, or their best friend moving away last year) in their list. Don't limit the list, instead point out the strengths they have shown in coping with past losses. The list may appear frightening or overwhelming to you, especially if it is long, but just read through it one item at a time. Your children may also refuse to make the list at all or say they can't think of anything. Tell them this is okay and give them permission to bring up any concerns or questions they have later on.

Teach Your Children How to Express Feelings Appropriately

Encouraging your children to express themselves does not mean you become a verbal punching bag for your children. If your children repeatedly call you names, swear, or verbally attack you, you need to place some limits on how they express their feelings. Let them know that while it is okay for them to tell you they are angry it is not acceptable for them to call you names. Tim's seven-year-old son Reggie told him to "shut up" when Tim told him he couldn't go camping with his friend Tom the following weekend. Tim said to Reggie, "My rule is that you don't say shut up. You can say, "I feel angry when you tell me I can't go camping with Tom this weekend." Redirect inappropriate expressions of feelings such as name-calling. Teach your children more productive, positive ways of verbally expressing their feelings. Model positive expression of feelings yourself. ("When you call me names, I feel hurt," or, "I understand that you are angry but when you say that word I feel disrespected by you.") Keep in mind your child's response to this may be something such as, "You didn't care about my feelings when you got the divorce. Why should I care how you feel?" Assure your child you understand that the divorce is difficult for him or her. Remember that appropriate expression of feelings is a skill your children must learn. My son said to me, after I had said something inappropriate to him in anger, "You're a grown-up and if you can't control what you say when you're angry, how am I supposed to know how to do it when I am only nine?" If you are having difficulty responding neutrally to your children's anger, practice exercises 8 and 10 (this chapter). Demonstrate patience in teaching your children to label and express feelings in a positive manner; understand that their initial attempts may not be successful. (Chapter 6 discusses helping your children express anger in more detail.)

Throughout the divorce, continue to tell your children you love them. The following exercise can provide an opportunity for your child to accept that you still love him or her.

EXERCISE 11: HOW WE SHOW OUR LOVE

Do this exercise with your child.

Materials

large piece of heavy-duty drawing or construction paper

scissors, glue sticks, markers

old magazines that have lots of pictures of people smiling, hugging, having fun together (parenting magazines, often for sale in libraries, work well)

Step 1. Tell your child that you love him or her and that together you are going to make a picture showing *how* you love each other.

Step 2. Go through the magazines together and ask your child to cut out pictures that show love. If your child is too young to cut, ask him or her to point to the pictures for you to cut out. Do not judge whether you think the pictures do or don't show love. Your child may pick out pictures of food or animals—this is okay.

Step 3. Have your child glue the pictures on the paper. Point to a particular picture that your child has pasted and ask him or her to tell you about it. Don't agree or disagree, just listen. Talk about how you show your child you love him or her.

Step 4. If your child is old enough, have him or her add words to the picture that describe love.

Step 5. Ask your child where he or she would like to hang the picture. Give your child a hug.

Continue to Hold Weekly Family Meetings

Continuing to hold family meetings on a weekly basis will assure your children that you will continue to give them opportunities to express their thoughts and feelings. Both parents do not have to be present at future family meetings. If you feel the other parent's presence would be beneficial to your children, discuss this with the other parent prior to the meeting. If possible, hold the family meeting on the same day and at the same time each week. This will aid you in consistently holding these meetings. At each meeting, review the calendar for the week. Let your children know when they will see the other parent and when they will return to your home. At each subsequent meeting make sure you finish talking about anything you were unable to at the last meeting. Refer to the list of questions and concerns your children have made (earlier in this chapter) and ask them if they have anything to add to their lists. Follow the tips below to assist you in using family meetings to facilitate communication in your family.

Tips for Successful Family Meetings

1. Continue to use weekly family meetings to:
   - facilitate communication between family members
   - talk about family issues, values, rules, chores, and complaints
   - review the weekly calendar
   - plan family activities.

2. Follow through on agreements reached during family meetings.

3. Set a time to start and stop the meeting and stick to it.

4. Keep a log of what is discussed and agreed upon in the family meetings.

5. Rotate the chairperson and secretary.

6. Parents should model the use of "I" messages.

7. If members are having difficulty listening to each other and talking all at once, use a "talking turtle" to help members take turns talking. A talking turtle is an object such as a stuffed turtle that the family member who is talking should hold. When the family member is done talking, he or she passes the turtle to another member. Only the person holding the turtle can talk.

8. End each family meeting by having everyone say something positive that is happening in their lives, or say something positive to each family member.

Children, particularly young children, tend to act out instead of verbalizing feelings. Your children may express their feelings through temper tantrums, bed wetting, lying, fighting, stealing, stomachaches, or headaches. (Chapter 7 gives more specific reactions by age.) Suppressing their feelings may intensify your children's acting out. Although it may be difficult for you to talk to your children about the divorce, talking is easier than trying to fix problems created by failing to do so. Giving your children opportunities to verbalize their feelings and modeling appropriate expression of feelings can reduce your children's tendency to act them out.

Normalize Your Children's Lives

The fear of change can be one of your children's greatest worries, so try to keep their lives as normal as possible. Assure your children they are still part of a family, even though the family has changed. It is important that your children have a sense of belonging and stability. Continue, as much as possible, to observe family traditions such as going to church, camping at the lake, taking Sunday drives, or driving around every December to look at the Christmas lights. Ester, mother of five, was concerned about how the divorce would affect their annual camping trip. "At first I was really worried about our first vacation without Tim, but as we planned it I realized how much Tim hated those family camping trips. He was always miserable and complained about everything. It was really freeing to know that we could do whatever we wanted to without worrying about whether Tim was going to gripe about it." Family traditions may feel different to you and your children without the presence of the other parent but they are important to your family's recovery. If you keep the lines of communication open, the changes that do occur will be less traumatic and your relationship with your children will continue to grow stronger.

KEY POINTS

- Children, like adults, tend to go through stages in their recovery from divorce.
- Feelings of anger, sadness, relief, and guilt are normal.
- Role model appropriate expression of feelings.
- Use indirect forms of communication to help your children express their feelings.

The feelings of abandonment triggered by a divorce can be even more acute than the loss triggered by a parent's death. Children not only lose daily contact with both parents, they may also lose the support of family, friends, or neighbors who may take sides or keep their distance rather than help support the children through the loss. To help alleviate the stress and unhappiness caused by separation, parents need to acknowledge, accept, and talk patiently with their children about their feelings. With support from you and the other parent, your children will know that they are not alone in this, that their feelings are normal, and that they have permission to express their feelings.

Children's Stages of Grief

Children, like adults, tend to go through stages in their recovery from divorce. The following discussion about these stages should not be interpreted as step-by-step instructions on how to grieve, but rather as guidelines to help you understand the emotional process that takes place during divorce. Keep in mind that your children (and you) may skip a stage or may shift back and forth between these stages.

Grieving takes a lot of energy, so don't be surprised if your children appear lethargic or do not feel like going to school, doing homework, or playing with friends. If these behaviors persist or if your child appears stuck at a particular stage in the grief process, you may want to talk to the school social worker or counselor or consult with a therapist who specializes in children of divorce. (Therapy is discussed in greater detail in chapter 13.)

Keeping communication open will help you determine which stages your children are in and what they need from you at various stages. Don't tell them how they should or shouldn't grieve. Grieving is a very individual process and, like adults, each child grieves in his

6

Understanding and Helping Your Children Express Their Feelings

or her own way. Some children grieve by crying, some don't cry at all. Some will want to talk, others will want to be left alone. To demonstrate that you are there for them, even if they say they want to be left alone, avoid asking a lot of questions and use reflective listening to let your children know that you are listening. For example, "I noticed that you're spending a lot of time in your room. Thinking about all of the changes in our family must be difficult for you." Listen to your children and stay in close contact with them as they work through their grief. This will help you understand how they deal with pain and will strengthen your relationship with them. Observing how they deal with the pain of divorce can also help you be more attuned to their emotional well-being throughout the remainder of their childhood and adolescence.

Shock

"It was kind of weird when Mom and Dad first told me about the divorce. I wasn't really upset, I just felt kind of numb" (Brian, fifteen). The first stage in the grief process of divorce is shock. Children may be stunned when you tell them about the divorce. Their eyes may appear glazed. They may appear calm, as if nothing has happened. This does not mean that they are not affected by the divorce. It may mean that the reality of the divorce is too painful. Shock is a defense that helps us deal with overwhelming, traumatic events by numbing our feelings until we gradually are able to cope with the situation.

Your children need for you to be patient through this stage. Help them through the stage of shock by talking to them about the divorce. Instead of using questions that can be answered with a yes or no, such as, "Are you mad that Mom and I are getting divorced?" use open-ended "I wonder" statements such as, "I wonder how your feeling about . . . " or, "I wonder if you are mad about . . ." Ask them what questions they have about the divorce or what will be happening. Do not, however, flood them with questions. Children, particularly adolescents, feel as though they are in an inquisition if parents ask too many questions. After asking a question, patiently wait until they answer before making a comment or asking another question. Parents are sometimes uncomfortable with silence but your children may need time to think about how they are feeling and how to put this into words.

Denial

"When Mom first moved out, I just said to myself that this was just another one of their fights and she'd be back soon" (Simone, twelve). Many experts combine the stages of shock and denial. In this stage, children may mask their feelings about the divorce and/or pretend that it is not happening. They may refuse to talk about it and say that they don't have any questions about it. Some children avoid telling their friends about the divorce or make up stories about the whereabouts of the absent parent. Others leave the room when parents start to talk about it. Younger children may put their fingers in their ears and hum or say, "I can't hear you!" when the subject of divorce is brought up. They may only want you to read stories to them about happy, intact families. They may draw pictures of all of you living happily together, or put Barbie and Ken in the same bed. This play is normal and can help them work through their feelings. You don't have to tell them that Barbie and Ken don't live together anymore. Most children will, with time, begin to accept that you are divorcing. Keep in mind that denial is a normal stage in the grief process and provides short-term relief from stress. It is a way for children to deny the reality of the divorce until they can better cope with the loss.

Your children may invent elaborate stories to try to get parents back together. They may pretend that they're sick so that the other parent will come back home. They may ask Dad to take Mom out to dinner or tell you how much the other parent misses you. "Dad is so depressed, he cries all the time. I know he's sorry for what he did. If you would just give him another chance, I know he'd come back home" (Taylor, fourteen). If children believe that their parent left because they were bad, they may try to be overly helpful and well behaved so that their parent will return. It is normal for children to have what experts refer to as reunification fantasies in which children dream about their parents getting back together. Your children may spend time daydreaming about the good times you had as a family. If your children's teachers report that your children are having trouble focusing in class, they may be daydreaming about your family, both the good and bad times. If this happens tell your children that you understand that this is difficult for them and encourage them to talk about what is bothering them.

Prolonged denial may be a result of your children blaming themselves for the divorce, or it may be an attempt to avoid persistent feelings of guilt, abandonment, or anger. If your children persist in trying to get you and your former partner back together, tell them something like, "Dad/Mom and I are getting a divorce because we are unhappy living with each other, not because we are unhappy with you. We are not getting a divorce because of anything you did and nothing you do will get us back together. You may have heard us arguing about you, but most parents, even ones who don't get divorced, sometimes argue about their children. Being good may make you feel better and I appreciate your help, but it won't get Dad/Mom and I back together." This may be difficult for your children to hear but they need to be reassured that they did not cause the divorce.

Although denial helps children through the initial phases of divorce, it does not provide a method of coping with the reality of divorce. Some children five to ten years after the divorce have still not accepted that the divorce is permanent. In the long term, denial may interfere with your child's ability to cope with issues that may surface in the future. If children continue to appear overly eager to convince you that they are okay, this could be a warning sign that they are denying their feelings about the divorce or they are worried that expressing these feelings would upset you.

Anger

"Sandy was so nasty towards me after Greg left. She accused me of driving her dad away. She'd tell me that she hated me and tell her little brother that if he wasn't such a brat, Dad would never have left" (Monica, mother of two). As the initial shock and denial wear off and reality sets in, your children may start to feel very angry about the divorce. They may feel that life isn't fair. Their lives are being dramatically disrupted and they don't like it.

Divorce, unlike death, accidents, or any natural disaster, results from a voluntary decision made by one or both parents. Children know that one or both parents have made this choice. They feel angry at their parents, who they feel are supposed to protect them, for disrupting their lives and creating the unhappiness they are experiencing. They may view one parent as immoral, selfish, uncaring, or inept at keeping their family together. At the same time, because they love and need their parents, they may feel guilty about being angry with them and have difficulty expressing it.

Children may express anger openly or covertly. They may scream, throw things, or hit friends or family members. They may act out their anger by engaging in dangerous behavior, stealing, lying, refusing to do what you ask them to, or running away. Grades may drop or your children may skip school. They may quit doing chores or stop associating with friends who they think are liked by their parents. Hanging out with the wrong crowd or shaving their heads can be a way of expressing anger—or it can simply be a way for your children to express their individuality. Don't assume that their desire to get a tattoo or pierce their nose is due to the divorce. Watch for sudden changes in your children's personality and keep talking to them about the divorce.

Sadness or Depression

Mourning begins after the initial shock and denial have worn off. Anger may continue or it may be replaced by a deep sense of sorrow. Your children have not only lost a parent, they have lost a way of life. They may feel helplessness and hopelessness and may think, "What's the use?" They may obsess about the absent parent. They may want to wear clothing or jewelry that belongs to the other parent. Some may act like the other parent or repeat phrases that the other parent frequently uses. Sometimes pretending that they are the other parent helps them deal with the loss.

They may also ask the same questions over and over. Hearing you answer the same questions repeatedly can help them deal with the loss, so approach these questions with patience and understanding and use reflective listening to assist you in helping them identify and express their feelings.

Healing

"My parents don't love each other but they still love me" (Carla, six). Healing begins as your children resume normal activities and are more able to talk about the reality of divorce. Healing will take at least two to three years. Your children will need to experience family holidays, birthdays, and other recurring family traditions with your changed family. Healing will be influenced by the conflict between their divorced parents and the relationship between the children and their parents. Parents can facilitate healing by reducing the conflict they have with each other, by cooperatively coparenting, and by developing a positive supportive relationship with their children.

Healing has started to occur for teens and young adults when they are willing to take a chance on love, when they accept that they are loved and capable of loving. Even though young adult children know that there is a chance that their own marriage will end in divorce, they can still be open to developing committed trusting relationships. Healing means believing in marriage and fidelity. It means feeling confident that I won't make the same mistakes my parents made. It is knowing that I can communicate with the people I love and develop my own healthy relationships.

Typical Feelings Experienced by Children of Divorce

Children experience a wide variety of feelings as they go through divorce, some of which are listed below. (How to help your children deal with their feelings is described by age group in the next chapter.)

Anger

"You're selfish. I don't want to have no daddy" (Emily, five). Your children want their home to be stable and consistent. They resent the change, even if you view it as positive. You promised to always be together and you broke that promise.

Your children may be angry at both parents or only one. Often children blame the parent who filed for the divorce. They do not know or understand the circumstances that created the problems. Sometimes, children may only express anger at one parent even though they may be angry with the other parent or both parents. One six-year-old child I worked with blamed the judge. Try not to take it personally when your child yells at you for something the other parent did such as being late for parenting time. Sometimes children are afraid that if they are angry with or express anger at one parent, that person may leave and not come back. So they express their anger at the parent that they feel safest with, secure in the knowledge that this parent will not reject them for it.

Rather than using your energy to justify your decision to divorce, help your children label their feelings and assist them in taking action to feel better. Children need time to work through their anger. They need to accept that parents aren't perfect, that like everyone else they make mistakes. They need to forgive their parents and themselves for being angry. Do not try to talk your children out of being angry. Think about how it felt the last time someone told you that you shouldn't get mad about something—it probably made you even angrier. Instead of telling your children not to get upset, let them know that it is okay to feel angry and teach them ways of expressing their anger that won't hurt themselves or others or damage property. Listed below are some healthy things you and your children can do when you are angry.

Count to ten

Take three deep breaths

Do something physical: push-ups, a walk, or bike ride

Sing a mad song

Do a mad dance

Read

Blow out your anger

Punch a pillow

Say, "I'm angry!"

Write down what you're angry about

Sadness, Abandonment, and Loss

When asked what he lost in the divorce, ten-year-old Evan responded, "My parents, my parent's love, and my family things." Divorce is a loss and your children must grieve this loss. Their sadness may be expressed through crying, moodiness, sleeplessness, restlessness, difficulty concentrating, feeling empty, play inhibition, compulsive overeating, or somatic complaints such as headaches or stomachaches, for which no physical basis can be established.

Your children will also experience secondary losses from the divorce such as loss of income resulting from the family having to support two separate households or loss of friends due to having to move or change schools.

To aid your children in feeling lovable and worthy, arrange for frequent contact with both parents. Assist them in accepting that the divorce is not their fault and help them build their self-esteem.

Fear

Jeremy, fourteen, asked his mother if he could return to treatment because he worried a lot and needed to talk about his relationship with his father. I had seen Jeremy in counseling two years prior to this, shortly after he and his mother moved out of the family home. Jeremy, who had come from a middle-class family, spent a great deal of time worrying about his mother and her ability to pay the bills. He asked me how much the therapy was going to cost his mother and physically relaxed when I informed him that the insurance would cover most of the cost. As therapy progressed, Jeremy shared with me that his father had told him that he was not going to help pay for Jeremy's college education. His father did, however, plan on paying for Jeremy's brother's education. At Christmas and birthdays his father demonstrated further discrepancies by buying Jeremy's brother a computer, Nintendo, a TV, and other electronic equipment while buying Jeremy clothes. The father's explanation for this was that since Jeremy's brother chose to live with him and Jeremy chose to live with his mother, he felt that Jeremy should get college money and other items from her. Both Jeremy and his father knew that his mother, who was working at a fast-food hamburger chain, could not afford expensive gifts and would be able to contribute very little to Jeremy's continued education. Jeremy's father, despite his denial that he was punishing Jeremy for choosing to live with his mother, was reinforcing Jeremy's fear that not only would he be unable to attend college but his current needs would not be met.

Children may have a heightened sense of vulnerability and anxiety during and following the divorce. They worry about whether their needs will be taken care of. These fears are intensified when a parent argues about finances and blames the other parent for lack of resources. Nothing may appear safe and secure for them. Younger children may fear that since one parent left, the other one will leave as well. "Who will take care of me?" or, "If you stopped loving Dad/Mom then you may stop loving me," are common worries. Sleep problems are often the result of children worrying that when they wake up in the morning they will be alone, abandoned by both parents. Continue to reassure and show your children that they are not alone and that they are loved.

Guilt

Many, but not all, children of divorce feel guilt over their parents' divorce. Young children may believe their misbehavior caused the divorce or that their fantasy wish of wanting one parent to go away magically made it happen. Children who were conceived prior to the marriage may blame themselves if they think that Mom and Dad got married because Mom was pregnant and not ready for marriage. They may think that Mom or Dad spent too much time with them and the other parent felt left out. They may have heard their parents fighting about them. "Mom wouldn't yell at Dad about the money if they didn't have to spend it on us" (Juan, ten).

Telling your children that the divorce is not their fault helps. Encouraging your children to talk about the divorce with you, with other adults, and with other children who have survived their parents' divorce can help them feel less guilty. Many schools and family agencies offer divorce groups for children that can assist your children in accepting that the divorce is not their fault.

Children may also feel guilty about the sense of relief they may feel when a parent moves out. They may be glad that the fighting has finally stopped but are also aware of the pain the divorce is causing one or both parents. They may feel guilty being happy or relieved, knowing that their parents are in emotional pain.

The most important thing to remember about feelings is that they are okay. They are an automatic, natural, normal part of being human. Feelings themselves do not get us into trouble or cause conflict in our relationships; the destructive behavioral expressions of these feelings are the cause. It can be difficult for parents to allow or even encourage their children to express feelings, especially anger. Keep in mind that children need to identify and express feelings so that they can develop appropriate coping mechanisms to adjust and effectively cope with the divorce. Children need assistance in learning to express and cope with their feelings in ways that will help them heal and won't hurt other people. Children, like adults, may have difficulty controlling the expression of feelings until they first recognize and acknowledge these feelings.

"After the divorce, it seemed like Isaac developed a split personality. One minute he was sweet and affectionate and the next he was swearing and throwing things at me. I used to tell him to take his evil clone back where it came from and bring my son back" (Kalee, mother of six). Children often have difficulty talking about divorce. When angry, sad, or upset, they express their feelings by acting up in school, throwing temper tantrums, complaining of stomach- or headaches, or wetting the bed. When asked what is troubling them, they may respond with a shrug of the shoulders. Use the next exercise to help your children identify and express their feelings.

EXERCISE 12: HOW AM I FEELING TODAY? CREATING A FEELING POSTER

Materials

Colored pencils, markers, or crayons

Large poster board

Glue stick

Scissors

Old magazines with pictures of people expressing various emotions

Step 1: Tell your child that together you are going to make a feeling poster. Explain to him or her that feelings are normal and that you care about his or her feelings. Explain that understanding and talking about our feelings helps us express those feelings in positive ways.

Step 2: Write or have your child write at the top of the poster board, "How Am I Feeling Today?"

Step 3: Have your child choose a feeling from the list below. Encourage a mixture of pleasant and painful feelings.

Abnormal	Confused	Enthusiastic
Abused	Considerate	Excited
Accepted	Content	Foolish
Alone	Cool	Friendly
Amused	Crabby	Frightened
Angry	Crappy	Funny
Annoyed	Cuddly	Furious
Anxious	Daring	Gay
Ashamed	Deceived	Glad
Awful	Delighted	Gloomy
Awkward	Deserted	Grateful
Badgered	Desirable	Greedy
Beautiful	Different	Grouchy
Brave	Dirty	Guilty
Capable	Disappointed	Happy
Caring	Doomed	Hassled
Cheated	Double-crossed	Heartbroken
Close	Ecstatic	Helpful
Clumsy	Embarrassed	Helpless
Comfortable	Empty	Hopeful
Confident	Enraged	Horrified

Hurt	Peaceful	Stubborn
Important	Picky	Stupid
Innocent	Powerful	Successful
Insecure	Proud	Tender
Insulted	Puzzled	Tense
Joyful	Quiet	Terrific
Joyous	Regretful	Terrified
Lazy	Rejected	Tired
Left out	Relaxed	Tolerant
Liked	Relieved	Torn
Lonely	Rotten	Tortured
Lost	Safe	Trapped
Loved	Satisfied	Trustful
Lucky	Screwed up	Uncertain
Misunderstood	Secure	Uncomfortable
Mixed up	Selfish	Understanding
Moody	Separated	Understood
Needed	Shy	Unloved
Nervous	Silly	Unwanted
Numb	Skeptical	Valued
Offended	Smart	Wonderful
Ornery	Sneaky	Worried
Overjoyed	Sorry	Worthy
Patient	Strong	

Step 4: Have your child draw a face of someone feeling that feeling, or have him or her cut out a picture from a magazine of someone who feels that way. To facilitate this process, you can go through the magazines by yourself ahead of time and tear out pictures of people feeling a variety of feelings. Your child can then choose from the pile you have already torn out.

Step 5: Instruct your child to glue the picture to the poster board.

Step 6: Instruct your child to write the feeling word under the picture.

Step 7: Repeat steps 3–6 until you have filled the board.

Step 8: Hang the poster in your child's room.

Step 9: Each day ask your child how he or she is feeling today. Ask him or her to point to the picture that represents that feeling.

Step 10: Role model expression of feelings by pointing to a picture on the poster and telling your child, "This is how I'm feeling today." You can also say, "This is how I feel when I get a hug from you," "This is how I feel when I fall down and scrape my knee," or "This is how I felt when my friend Sha moved away."

Role Model Appropriate Expression of Feelings

> *"Children have never been very good at listening to their elders, but they have never failed to imitate them."*
>
> —James Baldwin

Although it may be upsetting for children to see their parents angry, sad, afraid, or even relieved, it doesn't have to be harmful to them. Use these opportunities to role model appropriate expression of feelings. If your children see you crying, label your feeling and assure them that these feelings are normal. For example, "I'm very sad about the divorce, it's okay to feel sad when you lose something that is important to you." Do not blame your feelings on your spouse or your children. Adults and children need to take responsibility for their feelings. For example, instead of saying, "I wouldn't have to worry about these bills if your father would just pay his support on time!" say, "I am worried about how I'm going to pay the bills and that's why I'm going back to school. I hope to get my nursing degree so that I can get a job that will allow me to support our family." When you blame others for your feelings, you take away your power to change them and teach your children to be victims. Owning your feelings teaches your children to empower their feelings and take the necessary action to improve their lives. Assure your children that they are not the source of your unhappiness and that, with time, you will feel better. If you are upset with your children, use an "I" statement (chapter 5) to express how you feel and what you want changed. For example, "I am disappointed in you for hitting your sister and I would like you to tell her that you are mad at her rather than hitting her."

Do not go into detail with your children about your feelings, because doing so can be overwhelming and confusing. Instead, tell them what you plan on doing to feel better: "I am crying because I'm feeling sad. I'm going to take a bath to help me relax and feel better," or, "I am very angry. I'm going to go for a walk to cool off." In your Personal Notes section at the back of this book, make a list for yourself of things you do to cope with painful feelings. Help your children make their own list of what they can do to feel better when they are sad, angry, or scared. This will teach your children how to cope with their feelings.

Since children tend not to specifically express how they are feeling, parents can use indirect forms of communication with them, such as telling and writing stories, coloring and drawing pictures, and writing poems (particularly appealing to adolescent girls). This allows them to safely distance themselves from the situation. Provide a less threatening means of expressing and working through your children's feelings by telling them about other children who experience similar thoughts and feelings. Explain to them what these children do to cope with divorce. "I noticed that Lucas, whose parents are also divorced, is still playing on your basketball team. I'll bet playing ball with his friends helps him feel less lonely," or, " I always see your friend Megan with a book in her hands. Her parents are divorced too. I wonder if reading helps her keep her mind off of the divorce."

Building Your Children's Self-Esteem

Keep in mind the acronym CEASES when trying to build your child's self-esteem: Confidence, Encouragement, Accomplishment, Satisfaction, Effort, and Success. Adhering to the following techniques will help you build your children's self-esteem.

- Praise your children. Praise should be based on specific accomplishments that your child has achieved. Say, "I like the way your braided your hair," instead of, "You look pretty." (The use of praise is discussed in greater detail in chapter 10.)

- Communicate to your children that their thoughts and feelings are important. Don't say, "You shouldn't feel that way."

- Clearly establish and enforce rules and limits. Allow for flexibility when appropriate rather than basing it on your own frustration or guilt.

- Be a positive role model by taking pride in your own accomplishments, taking care of yourself, and learning from (and forgiving yourself for) your mistakes.

- Teach your children how to make decisions. Assist them in learning about time and money management.

- Be realistic in your expectations of your children. Take into account their age, and help them set obtainable goals so that they are successful. Ask them what their goals are for school and support them in taking steps to achieve those goals.

- Assist your children in accepting that it is okay to be different. Support them in being proud of their uniqueness.

- Support your children in being responsible. This will help them feel that they are valued. As they get older give them increased responsibility and freedom. This will reinforce your faith in their decision making.

- Show your children that they are loved by spending time with them and by hugging them.

- Demonstrate that what your children do is important to you by attending their activities such as school functions and award ceremonies. Talk to them about what's going on in their lives.

- When disciplining, focus on your child's behavior, not character. Distinguish between what your child does and who he or she is.

- Talk to your children about your own values and beliefs and your life experiences that shaped those values.

- Have faith in your children and use words of encouragement that communicate to your children that you believe in them.

- Set aside a place to show off your children's accomplishments. A trophy case, bulletin board, or even the refrigerator door can serve this purpose. Keep a scrapbook of your children's special drawings, school papers, and accomplishments.

- Help your children see mistakes as opportunities to learn rather than failures.

  "We are not retreating—we are advancing in another direction."

  —Douglas MacArthur

- When your children bring home school papers, point out the problems they got correct. Ask them what they did to get these problems right.

- Help your children learn new skills by breaking them down into simple steps that they can accomplish. As a soccer coach I don't focus on teaching children to play soccer. Instead, I teach them to dribble, pass, and shoot.

- Encourage your children to picture themselves accomplishing the task that they are trying to achieve.

- Encourage your children to help other people. Mowing a neighbor's grass, visiting someone in a nursing home, or collecting food for a soup kitchen can help your child feel worthwhile and needed.

- Say positive things about your children when talking to other adults. Do this when your children can hear you.

- Notice when your children do something right and let them know what attribute this demonstrates. For example, "That must have taken courage to jump off that high dive." Or, "You showed compassion when you hugged your brother after he got hit by that baseball."

- Immediately after your child has done something that you approve of, use phrases that build self-esteem such as:

Great job!	Super!
You deserve a hug!	You're special!
Thanks for being honest!	Exceptional idea!
You put a smile on my face!	That was a big help!
You're Number One!	You can do it!
Terrific!	Wonderful!
You're right!	You're a champ!
You're the best!	Wow!
Fabulous!	You're an angel!
Outstanding!	

In your Personal Notes section at the back of this book, write three positive things each of your children has done in the past week and then tell these things to your children to let them know you've noticed.

If you are concerned about your child's expression of feelings or if your child is having difficulty coping with the divorce, consider taking him or her to a therapist. How to know when your children need to see a therapist and how to find a therapist is discussed in chapter 13.

7

Age-Specific Reactions
to Divorce

KEY POINTS

- Children of divorce who are similar in age tend to have similar reactions and needs.
- Children regardless of their ages experience a broad range of thoughts and feelings that are at times not age-specific.
- Minimize changes for infants.
- Toddlers need frequent contact with both parents.
- Preschoolers need help in expressing feelings and reassurance that the divorce is not their fault.
- Reassure early school-age children that they will be taken care of.
- Avoid pressuring children ages nine to twelve to take sides or take on more responsibility than they can handle.
- Talk to teenagers and young adults about how the divorce affects them.

The effect of divorce on children depends on their age and sex, the relationship with their parents, the memories of their predivorce family life, and the manner in which their parents talk to them about the divorce.

A *general* description of the needs and common problems of children experiencing divorce at certain ages follows. However, parents need to be flexible, keeping in mind that children, regardless of their ages, experience a broad range of thoughts and feelings that are at times not age-specific. Also, since children mature at different rates and often regress during divorce, your children may exhibit behavior typical of a child at a different age. Read the descriptions of the children in all of the age groups and pay particular attention to the age group just below or just after your child's age group. These descriptions may provide clues to how your child may react to the divorce, and will give you assistance in helping them cope with your divorce.

Birth to One Year: The Age of Trust

Who They Are

The foundations of basic trust are built in the first year of life. To build trust and form attachments, infants need consistency and familiarity. They need to wake up to the same faces and go to sleep with the same voices singing familiar lullabies. Babies are not born with what is called "object permanence." When a person or object disappears from their view it is gone. When you leave the room, you are gone forever. This is why the game peek-a-boo is fun for them: you magically disappear and reappear. When you repeatedly come to your children when they cry, they learn that you will come back when they need you and will not permanently disappear. This helps build trust and a sense of safety.

How They React to Divorce

"For the first eight months, Jenny was an easy baby. She only cried when she was tired or hungry. She slept through the night and took a two-hour nap in the afternoon. When Bob and I separated it was like I had a different baby. Jenny was cranky all the time and wouldn't go down for her nap. She would scream when I would drop her off at Bill's for the weekend. When I would pick her up, she would cling to me like a monkey and for the first few days after the visit she would cry every time I left the room. For a while I even wondered if Bob was abusing her, she was so upset. But I knew that even though he was a lousy husband, he had been a good dad. I guess part of the problem was that I had also returned to work and I know I wasn't in the greatest shape emotionally. After a few months, she started to get used to the schedule and was less fussy. I think all of us needed time to adjust to the change" (Margo, mother of one). Infants and toddlers experience pain each time they are separated from a parent. The changes in parenting time, work schedule, or a parent's emotional state during a divorce can prevent infants from feeling safe and secure. Infants may react to these changes by crying, clinging, and being irritable.

What They Need

As much as possible, minimize changes in the environment. For example, if your infant is in daycare, both parents should use the same daycare provider. Try to keep the same schedule for feeding and sleeping. Try to use the same brand of formula and baby food. Give your infant a lot of verbal and physical affection. Spend lots of time rocking, holding, and singing to your infant. Babies need frequent contact with both parents. To increase familiarity, both parents can wrap the child in the same blanket when rocking or sleeping, and can sing the same lullabies. Talk to the other parent about ways to provide consistency. Decide who is going to be responsible for pediatrician appointments and immunizations. Share with the other parent when your children reach developmental milestones such as taking their first steps or saying their first words.

Newborn babies, particularly premature babies, are very easily overstimulated. Avoid yelling or fighting in front of your infant. Use a very calming, neutral voice during transition time from one parent's home to the other. Take steps to reduce your own anxiety and tension (chapters 11 and 12 will assist you in decreasing stress and dealing with your feelings). In your Personal Notes section at the back of this book, write down ways that you can help your infant cope with your divorce.

Ages One to Three: The World Revolves Around Them

Who They Are

Toddlers are very self-centered. They learn the word "no" and use it frequently to communicate that they are becoming aware that they are separate from you. They are walking with increased coordination and speed and tend to get into everything. At the same time, they are still very dependent on adults and separation from adults is often traumatic. At the park, a toddler will run away from his mother to chase a puppy, only to suddenly stop in his tracks, search for his mother with a look of panic on his face, and come racing back, plunging himself into his mother's arms. Toddlers are also beginning to realize that there are boundaries and limits. Children in this age bracket also start to use transition objects such as a favorite blanket, doll, or stuffed toy to comfort themselves.

How They React to Divorce

Change is also difficult for toddlers. They fear separation, and transitions from one parent to the other can be very traumatic. They may be cranky or cry for the other parent. They may not want you out of their sight and may desperately cling to you when you try to leave them. They may also have trouble falling asleep or sleeping through the night.

What They Need

Do not take it personally if your toddler has a temper tantrum or cries when separated from the other parent. Missing the other parent does not mean that they don't love or need you. Babies and toddlers do not have an accurate sense of time, so separations can be terrifying and waiting a week to see the other parent may seem like forever. Frequent contact with both parents can help reduce their fear of separation. Give them time to adjust to the parenting-time schedule. Assure them that you love them and that you will take care of them. Acknowledge that you understand that they miss the other parent. Show them on the calendar when they will see or talk to the other parent.

To help them deal with the loss when you leave them, give them affection that they can "take" with them. For example, "Here's a hug and an extra to take with you to Mommy's/Daddy's."

Provide safe predictable limits and structure. Try to keep the same bedtime routine in both homes. Reading the same bedtime story and making sure your children have their favorite blanket or toy with them can help. In your Personal Notes section at the back of this book, write down ways that you can help your toddler cope with your divorce.

Ages Three to Five: The Age of Curiosity

Who They Are

> "Where four is, there dirt is also,
> And nails and lengths of twine,
> Four is Mr. Fix-it
> And all his tools are mine.
> Four barges into everything
> (Hearts too) without a knock.
> Four will be five on the twelfth of July,
> And I wish I could stop the clock."
>
> —Elise Gibbs

Preschool children like to try things out. They watch adults and ask lots of questions, because they are trying to make sense of their world. To young children, parental approval is very important. ("Did

I do good, Daddy?" "Watch me, Mommy!") Preschool children also wear their hearts on their sleeves. They don't hide their feelings and often embarrass adults by blurting out everything they think, including, "Look, Mommy, that man doesn't have any hair."

How They React to Divorce

Preschool children tend to experience three types of problems relating to their parent's divorce: pain caused by the separation from a parent, confusion over the cause of the separation, and stress induced by the upheaval in the family. Specific reactions include:

- fear of being abandoned
- feeling guilty, angry, frustrated, fearful, sad, or confused
- worrying about their safety or whether they are loved
- denial of the divorce and pretending that the missing parent is coming back
- blaming themselves for the divorce
- believing that their hostile thoughts or bad behavior caused their parents to break up
- experiencing reunification fantasies
- making futile attempts to reunite the parents
- overcompliance
- thinking, "I'm not good enough," or, "I'm bad"
- difficulty handling transitions
- regressing back to sucking a thumb or wetting or soiling their pants
- hitting peers or younger siblings

Some toddlers may masturbate as an outlet for anxiety. Some begin to throw temper tantrums or develop sleep problems. Since young children do not have a clear sense of permanence, they may also repeatedly ask you if Mommy or Daddy is coming back today after you have clearly explained that he or she will not be living with you anymore.

What They Need

Some parents avoid telling young children about the upcoming divorce because they want to protect them from undue pain. However, this silence usually makes matters worse. Even young children can sense that something is wrong and are often confused about what is happening in their family. To help lessen their confusion, provide opportunities for your children to talk about the divorce and ask questions. Give them permission to talk about the divorce and to feel angry, sad, scared, or happy about it. When they express their feelings, do not say, "That's silly," or, "Don't feel that way." If your children repeatedly ask if Daddy/Mommy is coming back, calmly repeat that the divorce is final and that Daddy/Mommy now lives in a new place. Let your child know when he or she will see the other parent again.

"I noticed that whenever Cindy was playing with her doll house the mother and father dolls were always yelling at each other and bashing each other in the head. At first I didn't understand where all of this violence was coming from because her father and I never hit each other. When I asked her about it, she told me the Mommy was mad at the Daddy for bringing the kids home late. I realized that she must have overheard us fighting about it. I thought she was too young to know what was going on, but I guess she knew how hostile her dad and I were towards each other" (Sandra, mother of a four-year-old girl).

Young children express their feelings indirectly. Because younger children have a limited vocabulary, they are less likely to talk about their feelings and need you to help them express their feelings in age-appropriate ways. Parents can help them by using indirect forms of communication such as reading stories about other children whose parents are divorcing. There are many good storybooks about children and animal characters that are going through divorce. (Additional Reading, at the back of this book, lists some of these.) When you notice that your children are upset, encourage them to draw or color pictures about how they are feeling or about what is happening to them. Give your children dolls, puppets, or Playdoh to assist them in working through their feelings. Watch and listen to your children as they play for clues as to how they are adjusting to the divorce.

Begin to give preschoolers a "feeling" vocabulary. Sit on the floor with your child and bang a drum or squish a ball of Playdoh and say, "I'm mad." Make a sad face and say, "I'm sad." Point to a picture in a magazine of someone who looks scared and say, "That boy looks scared. I wonder what he's scared about." Take advantage of everyday experiences to label feelings. If the girl in front of you in the grocery line is having a temper tantrum, turn to your child and say, "That girl sure looks mad." When you're watching *Sesame Street* together and Elmo is laughing, say, "Elmo seems happy. What do you think he's happy about?"

Young children need assurance that they did not cause the crisis and they cannot resolve it. Repeatedly communicate that you still love them, give them lots of physical affection, and assure them that you will take care of them. Let preschoolers and other children who are experiencing reunification fantasies know that it is normal for them to want their parents to get back together but that you don't think that this is going to happen. "I know that you wish Mommy would come back home, but sometimes wishes don't come true. Mommy lives in a different house. We both love you very much and you will see Mommy tomorrow."

You can also prepare your preschooler for the switch from each parent's home by playing games with them to illustrate the process of going back and forth. Put one chair on one end of the room and another at the opposite end. One chair is Mom's house and the other is Dad's. Have them carry their suitcase, pillow, or toys back and forth between the chairs. Say hello when they arrive at your chair and good-bye when they leave to go to the other chair. Move one of the chairs into another room to show your child that Daddy's house can't be seen when he or she is at Mommy's house and vice versa. You can also have the child sit in the chair as you go get them to bring them back to your chair. This illustrates that you will always come back to pick them up from the other parent's home. In your Personal Notes section at the back of this book, write down ways that you can help your preschooler cope with your divorce.

Ages Six to Eight: The Age of the Loose Tooth

Who They Are

Children ages six to eight are becoming more independent. They are starting to establish friendships with particular children and want to choose what clothes they wear. Six-, seven-, and eight-year-olds are content being six, seven, or eight. They no longer desire to be babies but they don't yet yearn to have the freedom of adolescence. They tend to play with children of their own sex. They love to tell their parents silly knock-knock jokes but often get the punch line wrong. They still have a strong need to cuddle and be held but kissing them in front of other children, particularly for boys, becomes taboo.

How They React to the Divorce

Josephine is a nine-year-old girl whose parents are in the middle of a long hostile court battle. When I asked her to make a collage of what was happening in her family, Josephine cut a picture of a girl out of a magazine, carefully cut off both of the girl's arms, and glued one arm on each side of the paper. She then glued the girl's body in the center. When I asked Josephine to tell me about the picture she said, "I feel torn in two. My mom is always telling me to tell Dad that he better send the support check. When I asked Dad to buy me some new clothes for school, he told me to tell Mom to quit spending the checks on herself and get me the clothes I need. I'm so sick of it. I wish they'd just leave me out of it. Don't they care how that makes me feel?"

As with younger children, kids in this group may blame themselves for the divorce. They think about being deprived of food or toys or being otherwise neglected. They frequently feel abandoned. They may be preoccupied with feelings of rejection, loss, loyalty conflicts, and guilt. They worry that they will forever lose the parent who has left the home. They may be afraid of being replaced: "Will Daddy get a new little girl?" Young girls may develop fantasies that their father will disappear and return after they are grown up. They often cry or are cranky, and feel empty and unable to concentrate at school. Because of their preoccupation with fighting and superheroes, they may see divorce as a battle in which they, like their Power Ranger heroes, must take sides. They yearn for the absent parent and often attempt to get their parents back together, even trying to set up dates by forging love notes from one parent to the other. (Remember the movie *The Parent Trap*?)

Children ages six to eight do not say that they are under stress. Problems coping with the divorce may show up in nervous habits such as nose-picking, hair-twisting, grimacing, stuttering, nail-biting, and pencil-chewing. They may withdraw, cry, become angry or aggressive, or become overly compliant.

If the reason for the divorce has not been explained to them, they will make up an explanation for it. Since they don't yet understand that there are two sides to every story, they may put the entire blame on one parent. If a parent begins dating soon after the initial separation, this person may be the one blamed.

What They Need

Because early school-age children have not yet developed the ability to think logically, explaining things calmly and rationally will not necessarily lead to understanding by children at this age. Use indirect forms of communication such as those described in chapter 6 to facilitate understanding. Like preschoolers, they continue to need help in labeling and verbally expressing feelings. Use techniques similar to those in the preschool section to help six- to eight-year-olds develop a "feeling" vocabulary. Put up a feeling poster (chapter 6) and ask your children every day how they are feeling today.

Sit down and look through magazines with your children. Point out pictures of people who look sad, angry, scared, or happy, and make comments about how you think that person may be feeling. Use "I wonder" statements to encourage them to talk about why the person may be feeling that way. For example, "That boy looks sad, I wonder why he's so sad." Then pause and wait to see if your child responds. Point to other pictures and ask your child how he or she thinks that child may be feeling.

Children ages six to eight also have a strong desire to please. Placing them in the position of having to tattle on or keep secrets from the other parent creates much anxiety, as they want to please both parents. Since they can experience divided loyalties, it is particularly important at this age for parents to avoid saying negative things about the other parent.

Early school age children need to be assured that they will be taken care of, that their needs will be met. Children living with single parents may also need reassurance that they are safe, that you have a plan to protect them from fire, bad guys, and monsters. If you do have to cut back because of financial restraints, assure them that they will have enough food and a safe place to live. In addition, children at this age continue to need lots of physical affection. Hug them and cuddle with them when they are not in front of peers. In your Personal Notes section at the back of this book, write down ways that you can help your six-to-eight-year-old cope with your divorce.

Ages Nine to Twelve: The Age of Accomplishment

Who They Are

Competence and confidence mark the last half of what is referred to as the middle years. Latency-age children want to be good at something and they compare themselves to other children. Competition and team sports become important.

For most adults, our first clear memories of childhood are from when we were between nine and twelve. We remember friendships and events that taught us life's lessons. We recall the rejection and embarrassment we felt at being the last one chosen to play baseball; the jokes, rhymes, and riddles we learned; and even the taste of the mystery meat in the cafeteria. The onset of puberty is a time when children socialize more outside the family and the opinions of peers become increasingly important. Children at this age begin to hide their feelings and don't like to cry in front of peers. They will develop best friends, and loyalty is very important. These children have an increased understanding of life and morality and can empathize with others.

How They React to Divorce

"I want my parents to stop fighting. I want my family back together again. I want to do things my way, no one else's, I want my stepmother to be able to talk to me if she has any problems, I want my parents to talk, not argue, I want to have too many things. I can't have what I want, because the world don't revolve around me!" (Kendra, twelve).

Divorce and remarriage is frequently most difficult on children from nine to twelve years of age. They begin to understand relationships within the family and they become more sensitive to family conflicts. Many children feel anger and shame over the divorce and they worry about the changes that will result. Anxiety is expressed by behavioral or academic difficulties in school. They sometimes become preoccupied with the divorce and have trouble concentrating at school. They may also get into fights or withdraw from peers. They may experience nightmares. They may be upset without knowing why. They experience feelings of anger, grief, anxiety, and powerlessness. Feelings of loneliness, loss, and deprivation can result in depression or other emotional problems. In the movie *Stepmom* the boy says to his mother about his new stepmom, "I'll hate her if you want me to." Since preteens tend to think in very black and white terms, they are susceptible to parents' attempts to pressure them to take sides.

Children at this age also worry about their parents. Preadolescents may try to take the place of the absent parent and try to act more mature than they are. They are becoming more aware of their parents' moods and wonder about their parents' ability to take care of them.

What They Need

Children ages nine to twelve need lots of opportunities to express their feelings, so listen and encourage the expression of these feelings. Help them label and understand their feelings. Talking to a child about peers whose parents are divorced provides opportunities for children to cope. For example, "I wonder what Courtney does to feel better when she misses her dad." Praise your children for their attempts to appropriately express their anger.

Since loyalty is important, avoid putting your children in a position of having to take sides. Say positive things about the other parent and give your children permission to have a relationship with the other parent. Do not argue in front of the children. Provide opportunities to build happy memories.

Assure your children that you are okay. If they see you crying, assure them that crying helps you feel better and that when you are done crying, you will do what it takes to feel better. Because you are now the only parent in the home, your children may have to be left home more often and they may have to help out more with household chores. Be careful not to put too much responsibility on preteens and teens too quickly. Gradually add additional responsibilities. Support them in resuming normal activities. Don't try to get them to ignore the divorce but encourage them to continue to remain involved with friends, school, and social activities. Allow them to continue to be kids and don't push them to grow up too fast. In your Personal Notes section at the back of this book, write down ways that you can help your nine-to-twelve-year-old cope with your divorce.

Ages Thirteen to Eighteen: The Age of Raging Hormones

Who They Are

> *"The young always have the same problem—how to rebel and conform at the same time. They have now solved this by defying their parents and copying one another."*
>
> —Quentin Crisp

> *"Oh to be only half as wonderful as my child thought I was when he was small, and only half as stupid as my teenager now thinks I am."*
>
> —Rebecca Richards

Adolescence is a time of physical, emotional, and social change. They can be self-conscious, idealistic, moody, rebellious, and filled with inner turmoil. Teenagers are forming their identity and making choices. I remember as an adolescent being told by an adult, "These are the best years of your life." I thought to myself, "Oh no. I can't stand it if it gets any worse." During adolescence, children begin to understand the different behaviors and attitudes of males and females. To adults, it seems they spend half their life talking on the phone. Spending time with friends is much more appealing than being with family yet they still need parental guidance. Adolescence can be a time of rebellion, but the stability of the family acts as a safety net for the testing of new experiences.

How They React to Divorce

"Nobody knows how hard these last few years have been for me" (Jenny, seventeen, whose parents divorced when she was thirteen). Parental divorce can be very painful and traumatic in adolescence. Teenagers may become hesitant about developing their own emotional relationships as a result. They may question commitment and fear that they will be hurt and that their own marriage will someday fail; they fear that they will repeat their parents' mistakes. They grieve the loss of family and childhood. They feel rejected by parents who may be too preoccupied with their own emotions to help them. They react to feelings of abandonment by turning away from home and relying even more heavily on peers for support. During a divorce, adolescents usually have increased responsibilities or are expected to act mature, and they may resent this if it interferes with time spent with peers. Teens worry about financial matters and their parents' emotional well-being. They experience many feelings of loss and anger. They may have trouble focusing in school, have physical complaints, or experience chronic fatigue. Their self-esteem may suffer and they may distance themselves from family even more than they normally would. The breakup of a family during adolescence weakens the safety net of the family that teens depend on for security, and they may suffer from depression as a result.

If teenagers are unable to discuss, understand, and accept the divorce, they may act out their feelings. This may take the form of engaging in dangerous modes of rebellion such as delinquent activities, skipping school, befriending peers who are already engaging in acting out, abusing alcohol and drugs, threatening or attempting to run away or committing suicide. Or, teens may hold back their feelings altogether due to fear of their parents' reactions. When Leslie's parents divorced, she was seventeen. Her parents were impressed, at the time, at how well Leslie appeared to be adjusting to the divorce. Leslie continued to participate in school and social activities, and never complained about having to take care of her younger bothers and sisters while her mother worked. Two years later, after her boyfriend broke up with her, Leslie fell apart. She stopped going to classes and ate very little. Her roommate was so worried about her, she called Leslie's mom. The loss of her boyfriend had triggered feelings of abandonment that she had buried at the time of the divorce. This delayed reaction has been referred to as the "sleeper effect" by Judith Wallerstein, who has done long-term studies on the effects of divorce on children.

What They Need

Teens need family structure, guidance, and protection. They need to find appropriate outlets for their feelings and encouragement from parents. Provide opportunities for your teens to talk about feelings, concerns, and complaints. Holding family meetings and engaging in one-on-one conversations with each parent is important. Writing poems, keeping a journal or diary, or writing letters to their parents that they can send, throw away, or keep helps teens express and understand their feelings. Drawing pictures of how they feel about the divorce can also help them work through their feelings and communicate their thoughts.

Be honest with your teenagers about the divorce without giving the details of the marital relationship. Loyalty is an issue at this age and parents should avoid encouraging teenagers to side with one parent. A teen who sides with the same-sex parent may become bitter toward the opposite sex. A teen who sides with the opposite-sex parent may experience problems with his or her identity and pride in being male or female.

Teens can start to understand that there are two sides to every story. Do not rely on them for emotional support. Encourage them to spend time with peers. Encourage friends to visit in both homes and be flexible when establishing parenting-time schedules to allow for school, hobbies, sports, and social activities. If your teenagers want to go to the other parent's home because of some extracurricular or social activity, let them know that they will have to discuss it with the other parent. I tell older teenagers that if they want the freedom to make changes in the parenting-time schedule, they have to take the responsibility of discussing it with their parents. This includes, if needed, making alternative arrangements for transportation. It is important, however, to also communicate that the parents, not the child, will make the final decision regarding parenting-time schedules. For children who have trouble making friends, sign them up for an adult-supervised peer activity such as a sporting, computer, or art class.

Preteens and teenagers, in particular, may have a difficult time seeing their parents date. Their own sexuality is beginning to emerge, and thinking about you as a person with sexual drives can be very confusing for them and may overstimulate their own sexual urges. It is difficult for children ages eleven and up to see their parents display affection toward members of the opposite sex. Give your teenagers time to adjust and get to know the person you are dating before displaying physical affection in front of your kids. Very gradually begin to start holding hands, hugging, or kissing in front of them and talk to your children about how this affects them.

Teenagers have a strong need to fit in and be accepted by peers. They already feel different and divorce can intensify feelings of isolation. Well-meaning school counselors, neighbors, or church members sometimes single these children out for special attention. While teens do need support and attention from these adults, adults also need to be sensitive to the reality that teens may reject this attention in an effort to conform to members of their peer group who are not receiving this attention.

Continue to provide clear, reasonable, and firm limits. Do not play into the game of, "If you don't let me I'm going to go live with

Dad/Mom." Don't let them avoid punishment, chores, or responsibilities by going to the other parent's house. In your Personal Notes section at the back of this book, write down ways that you can help your teenagers cope with your divorce.

Adult Children of Divorce: What Do I Want to Do?

Who They Are

Young adulthood, or, as called by some, "the age of secondary adolescence," is a time of choice. Young adults are making decisions about school, career, religion, marriage, friends, and politics. They begin to see their parents as real people and understand that parents aren't totally ignorant.

How They React to Divorce

Grown children, even those who have moved away or are raising their own families, are very much affected by divorce. Adult children will ask, "Why now?" It is hard for them to understand why the marriage can't continue if it has lasted this long. Young adults still need the safety net that parents supply. "My mom remarried right after I graduated from high school. I felt she couldn't wait until I went away to school so she could sell the house and move away with him" (Martha, twenty). The knowledge that no matter what happens they can always go home helps young adults take on the challenges of adulthood. Divorce disrupts this sense of security and may inhibit their willingness to take risks.

Relationships and trust become more difficult for adult children of divorce. Young adults may avoid long-term commitments to keep from getting hurt. Divorce shakes their sense of security: "When my parents divorced after thirty years of marriage, I learned that there was no such thing as a sure thing" (Joel, twenty). Young adults may worry about being betrayed and abandoned and/or may get into overly dependent relationships. They may choose someone who needs them so badly that they won't ever leave. This is particularly true if they view one parent in the divorce as the helpless victim of the other parent's desire to end the marriage. Young women may also become attracted to older men. These relationships feel safer, more reliable, and stable, providing a sense of being taken care of. Teenagers and young adults may make poor choices in their relationships as a result of lowered self-esteem. They settle for less because that is all they believe they deserve.

Single adults living away from home worry about which parent they will stay with during college breaks, and having to choose may make them angry. Married children have told me that it is difficult enough having to divide their time between in-laws, let alone having to visit Mom and Dad separately. Adult children continue to use their parents as role models and, like adolescents, may question the stability of their own marriage. I remember thinking, when my sister divorced after twenty-two years, "If she can't do it, how can I?" I worried that my own husband would, one day out of the blue, come home and say, "I'm not happy, I found someone new, and I'm leaving."

What They Need

Talk to adult children on an adult level and let them know that both parents contributed to the problems in the marital relationship. Explain that relationships are hard work and talk to them about how people change. Balance your explanation of the reality regarding what happened to cause the divorce with their need to feel hopeful and positive about relationships. To help your children develop positive relationships and give them hope for their own marriages, talk to them about what might have helped early on in your marriage. Discuss with them the three "Cs" of good marriages: communication, compromise, and conflict resolution. Talk to them about what they can do to make their own relationships successful, such as spending time with each other, acknowledging their partner's contributions, and avoiding taking the other partner for granted. Support young men in dealing with, rather than avoiding, their feelings about the divorce. Encourage them to talk about their fears and challenge their negative thinking. ("Since my father failed as a husband, I will too.")

Young adult children still need for you to support them in spending time with both parents so that they don't feel torn between the two of you. Like adolescents, they may still struggle with loyalty issues and are still forming their identity. They need for you to avoid complaining or putting down the other parent. Avoid putting them in the position of having to take sides by blaming the other parent. Blaming the other parent often backfires with adolescents and young adults—your children may feel that they have to defend the other parent and take his or her side. This results in the children becoming upset with you rather than dealing with the reality of their relationship with the other parent. At the same time, if the other parent has consistently not pursued a relationship with your children and has not visited them consistently, do not pressure your children to initiate contact. They need to develop a relationship with the other parent separate from your influence.

Do not use your children, even if they are adults, to ventilate your feelings about the other parent. Do not confide in them the specific details of the marital relationship. Your bad-mouthing the other parent can hurt your children even if they are adults. It can damage their self-image, their relationship with the other parent, and even their relationship with you.

Discuss with your adult children and your former partner how the holidays are spent. If your children have their own children, assure them that both parents will continue to have a relationship with their grandchildren. Your grandchildren need the unconditional love, the family history, and the wisdom of experience that grandparents can offer. Continue to attend your grandchildren's performances, school functions, and sporting events. Your children and grandchildren need your support now more than ever. In your Personal Notes section at the back of this book, write down ways that you can help your adult children cope with your divorce.

8

When You're Ready to Start Dating Again

"The hunger for love is much more difficult to remove than the hunger for bread."
—Mother Teresa

KEY POINTS

- Give yourself and your children time to adjust to the separation and divorce before you start dating.
- Until a serious relationship develops, restrict your dating, if possible, to times when your children are with the other parent.
- Allow your children to talk about their feelings toward you dating.
- Continue rituals that have been established.

In the early stages of the divorce process you may feel that you will never want to get involved with another man or woman, but as you recover from the divorce, your need to be in a loving relationship will grow again. This can be a scary prospect. It can also be a healthy way for you to get out and spend time with another adult. It can bring joy back into your life and help you begin living again. Your children, however, may not share your enthusiasm. Their reaction to your dating may range from joy to sadness and from indifference to outrage. Dating challenges their belief that you and the other parent will get back together. Your children may feel pushed out or unloved, and may resort to acting out to try to stop you from dating, which in turn may make you feel guilty and angry. There are, however specific things you can do to help your children accept your dating.

"The first time I brought Lucy home to meet my kids, they nearly crucified her. They started out with an inquisition into her personal life and then proceeded to tell her all of their mom's qualities that they were sure she didn't possess. Fortunately, Lucy was a good sport about it and after a lot of effort, time, and patience on her part, the kids eventually accepted her as a part of our lives" (Bob, now happily married to Lucy).

Give yourself and your children time to adjust to the separation and divorce before you start dating. And until a serious relationship occurs, parents should avoid dating openly. In the initial stages of a new relationship, try to limit your dating to the time when your children are with the other parent. This is particularly true if your time with your children is limited to less than four days per week. Karen, mother of two young children who spent every other weekend with their father, put it this way. "I'm glad I started dating again. But I'm also glad I only went out with Jim when my kids were with their dad. Jim was a lot of fun to be with. It felt good to know I could feel passionate about someone again. The last few years of my marriage I just felt numb and I was beginning to wonder if I'd ever have those feelings again. But I soon discovered that Jim drank too much, was immature, and not someone I could marry. I stopped seeing him after a few months. Since my kids never met him they didn't have to deal with our breakup."

If your children do not spend time with the other parent on a weekly or biweekly basis and you have to leave them with a babysitter while you go out on dates, let them choose which sitter they want from a list that you have preapproved. This can help reduce their resistance to you going out without them. Another alternative, if your children are open to it, is to arrange to have your children spend the night with a friend or favorite family member.

What to Look For in a Partner

"One who has not only the four Ss, which are required in every good lover, but even the whole alphabet; as for example . . . Agreeable, Bountiful, Constant, Dutiful, Easy, Faithful, Gallant, Honorable, Ingenious, Kind, Loyal, Mild, Noble, Officious, Prudent, Quiet, Rich, Secret, True, Valiant, Wise; the X indeed, is too harsh a letter to agree with him, but he is Young and Zealous."

—Miguel De Cervantes

Many divorced individuals begin to question their ability to choose a partner for themselves. They worry that they will make another mistake and choose the wrong partner. Use your experience to help you to make a more realistic, mature decision about choosing a life partner. One way of deciding if this relationship is worth pursuing is to make a list of your interests and values and another list of the interests and values of the other person. Circle the ones you have in common. Ideally, the number of ones circled should be greater than the ones not circled.

Use the next exercise to help you identify qualities to look for in a long-term partner. This exercise is not meant to be a checklist such as the kind you use to shop for a house or car; it is an exercise to stimulate thinking and help you identify what you want in a partner.

EXERCISE 13: MY PERFECT PARTNER

Listed below are qualities that divorced parents should look for in a potential long-term partner.

Keep in mind that no one is perfect and the person you are falling in love with may not have all twenty of these qualities. Be realistic in your expectations and patient if this person demonstrates a willingness to communicate and develop these attributes.

1. Supports my parenting style and rules.

2. Avoids being critical and does not tell my children or me what we should or shouldn't be doing.

3. Avoids comparing my children to his or her children or other children.

4. Understands my children's need to spend time alone with me without feeling jealous.

5. Is patient and understanding when plans have to be canceled or changed because of something that comes up with the children.

6. Talks to both my children and me, and treats us all with respect.

7. Avoids making sarcastic comments about my children or me.

8. Listens to and appears interested in what my children have to say.

9. Talks about the children in a neutral, nonjudgmental, nondefensive manner.

10. Demonstrates positive communication skills.

11. Avoids abusing alcohol or drugs.

12. Is willing to proceed slowly in his or her relationship with my children.

13. Enjoys family celebrations such as birthdays, holidays, and vacations.

14. Respects the boundaries I place on how much physical affection we display in front of the children.

15. Approaches my children's acting out in response to our dating with understanding and compassion.

16. Understands my feelings about my children and comforts me when I miss being with them.

17. Likes to do activities alone with me as well as ones that include my children.

18. Has fun and is comfortable interacting with my children and my children are comfortable and have fun with him or her.

19. Takes appropriate responsibility and apologizes when he or she has made a mistake with me or my children.

20. Able to forgive my children and me when we make mistakes.

In the Personal Notes section at the back of this book, write down what qualities are important to you. If you are currently dating, ask yourself which of those qualities describe the person with whom you are involved.

When a Relationship Becomes Serious

When a more steady relationship develops and you feel ready to introduce him or her to your children, adhere to the following guidelines to assist your children in adjusting to the change.

Continue to Spend Time Alone with Your Children

Your children may resent having to share your time and attention with another adult. They already feel a sense of loss over the divorce and may fear that your dating means that they will lose you too. Your children will be less likely to view this new person as a threat if you demonstrate that they are still important. Spend at least thirty minutes a day alone with each child. Plan longer outings such as going to a concert or renting a canoe for a couple of hours. Wednesdays, I usually work a twelve-hour day, so every Wednesday I take a break in the middle of the day and take my children out to lunch. It has become such a pattern over the past five years that, when my son's teacher sees me pull in the parking lot on Wednesdays, she says, "It must be Out to Lunch Day."

Slowly let your children get to know the person you are dating and gradually allow them to see you display physical affection toward each other. Denise came to see me because she was worried about how her children were reacting to her relationship with her boyfriend Kyle. "My children can't seem to stand seeing Kyle and I kiss, hug, or even hold hands. Their father and I never touched each other in front of the kids because it seemed we were always fighting or not talking to each other. I was hoping to show the kids that normal, happy couples show their affection towards each other. But whenever Kyle and I sit on the couch together, Stephanie, who is four, sits between us and starts whining. Margaret, who is fourteen, hides out in her room and tells me how gross it is the way Kyle and I are always pawing each other." As we talked, Denise started to understand that this change, even though she felt it was positive, was difficult for her children. Just seeing their mom with another man was a shock to Stephanie and Margaret. As Denise backed off on being physically affectionate and gave her children time to get to know Kyle, they became more comfortable around him. Stephanie still sits with them on the couch but she usually brings a book with her and, instead of whining, asks Denise or Kyle to read to her. Margaret doesn't hide in her room as much and, since finding out that Kyle is, like herself, a Chicago Bulls fan, she and Kyle have started watching the basketball games together.

Although your holding hands and kissing may feel very good to you, it is often upsetting for children. This is especially true of adolescents. Your children's sense of loyalty toward the other parent as well as reunification fantasies may create feelings of hostility toward the person you are dating. In addition, your children my be concerned that this person is trying to take the place of the other parent or that he or she may influence your parenting by adding new rules and restrictions.

Your children may also worry that this relationship will also break up and you and they will be hurt again. Janine brought her ten-year-old son Cody to see me because he had been stealing and was openly hostile toward her new boyfriend. Cody's parents were divorced three years ago and his mother's live-in boyfriend of two years had moved out two months ago. In addition Cody's brother had gone to live with his father. Cody had suffered three major losses in three years and his behavior was his way of keeping distance between himself and this new man, thus protecting himself from further loss and abandonment.

Allow Your Children to Talk About Their Feelings About You Dating

Instead of defending your right to date, use reflective listening (chapter 5) to open communication. If your children are rude to your date, talk to them when you are alone about how they are feeling. Communicate to your children that although they have a right to their feelings, you expect them to talk to the person that you are dating, as with anyone else, in a respectful manner. Reinforce your children's efforts to accept that you are dating.

Continue Rituals That Have Been Established

One of the reasons dating is difficult for children is that it is yet another change in all of your lives. Minimize the change by continuing family rituals such as eating meals together, saying prayers together, or watching Disney together on Sunday nights. If your dating interferes with one of these rituals modify it so that it still occurs. For example, if you are going out on a date and won't be home to put your children to bed, read them a bedtime story before you leave.

Dating can be a very difficult and painful process for your children or it can be an opportunity for both of you to grow and learn. As one mother put it, "Ten years after the divorce my thirteen-year-old son, Johnethan, said to me, 'I really think you should go out more, Mom. Just make sure the guy has a motorcycle, a full-time job, is a nice person, is good at sports, and likes kids'" (Kristi, mother of two teenagers).

9

Remarriage

"To keep a marriage brimming, with love in your loving cup. Whenever you're wrong, admit it; Whenever you're right, shut up."
—Ogden Nash

KEY POINTS

- Clarify roles.
- Discuss how decisions will be made and how money will be spent.
- Involve your children in the wedding ceremony.
- Communicate with each other.
- Compliment your partner and show appreciation.
- Establish a relationship separate from your family of origin and from previous relationships.

"Getting married again was a tough decision for me. Joe is a great guy and he's wonderful with my kids. But I had heard so many horror stories and because my first marriage was a disaster I was really gun shy. After three years I finally agreed to marry Joe and I'm glad I did. Joe and I have worked really hard at trying to understand each other's and our children's needs. We have our problems like any other family but we try to keep communication open. I'm glad my kids have had the opportunity to see that married couples can work out their problems without trashing one another" (Meredith, mother of four).

Judith Wallerstein, in a ten-year study, found that many second marriages were happier. She observed that many adults were able to learn from earlier experiences and avoid making the same mistakes. She saw much growth, especially in women, in competence and self-esteem. However, she also noted that feelings of anger, hurt, and humiliation often linger and some adults do not recover. Given the high rate of failure in second marriages, the decision to remarry needs to be thoroughly evaluated. As a general rule, most divorce counselors recommend waiting until three years after the divorce to remarry.

Before You Get Married

The following areas should be discussed prior to and throughout your marriage.

Clarify Roles

Decide together who will be doing the cooking, shopping, and cleaning. On the family calendar write down who will be transporting the kids to school, daycare, and so on. Talk about your expectations about rules and chores. Discuss who will be doing the discipline and what each of you believes to be appropriate discipline. Use Exercise 5 (chapter 3) to help you establish household rules. Talk about how each of you will support each other's role as an authority figure: "I will not disagree with a judgment you make regarding the children in front of them. If I disagree with you, I will discuss this with you in private." You should also discuss your thoughts and feelings about each other's careers and expectations regarding working outside and at home.

Despite What Your Grandmother Told You, You Should Talk About Sex and Money

Discuss what each of you expects regarding how financial decisions will be made. My husband and I agreed when we first got married that neither one of us would spend more than fifty dollars, outside of the regular household bills, without first discussing it with each other. We have modified this amount as our income changed, but talking about finances before the money is gone has helped us avoid numerous arguments. Talk about your goals and plans for retirement. Discuss who will be paying which bills. Discuss how financial decisions will be made regarding the children, such as school and college tuition, school activities, clothing, books, toys, and so on. Financial issues are discussed in further detail in the next chapter, which includes an exercise on using allowances to motivate children to do chores.

Talk about birth control. Discuss your medical history and how current or past medical problems may influence your sexual functioning. Talk about how and when you enjoy having sex. You should also talk about whether you plan on having children together.

Involve Your Children in the Planning of the Wedding

"My dad told us that he was getting remarried the week before the ceremony. I felt like I wasn't important enough to warrant him letting me know sooner. It put a crimp in the relationship between my stepmom and me right from the start" (Jacob, twenty-two). Your children need time to talk about how your getting remarried will affect them. Say something like, "I have found someone I can love and live happily with. I have decided to marry him or her."

Explain to your younger children what a stepparent is. Discuss his or her role in the family. For young children, use a simple explanation such as, "A stepparent is a grown-up who, just like you, loves me." Assure your children that this person will not take the place of their father or mother. He or she will be another adult with whom they can talk.

"I almost gave myself an ulcer worrying about how I was going to tell Angela that Ted and I were planning on getting married. But when we told her that we wanted her to be the flower girl, she was so excited. All I heard for the next two weeks was, 'When are we going to go get my dress?'" (Margaret, mother of a five-year-old girl).

Having all of your children and your future spouse's children participate in the planning and wedding ceremony will assist them in accepting the marriage. Even if you are planning a small ceremony, give each child something to do (being your best man or maid of honor, seating the guests, doing a spiritual reading, or passing out rice, bubbles, or birdseed to the guests after the ceremony).

Plan the honeymoon so that you spend part of it with them and part of it alone with your new spouse. Jetaime, mother of two, took her sister and her children with her to Disney World on her honeymoon. She and her new husband stayed in one hotel and her sister and the children stayed in another. They all went to the attractions together for the first three days and then she and her husband went off by themselves for the remainder of the week while her sister took the children to other attractions.

What Makes a Marriage Work

Although choosing the right partner is important, successful marriages are hard work and are built over time. Good marriages are built on understanding, negotiation, and compromise. The work and time that it takes to have a relationship with your spouse that is nurturing, supportive, and emotionally and sexually gratifying is worth the effort. The following guidelines will help you strengthen the relationship between you and your new spouse and assist you in having a long and satisfying marital relationship.

Communicate with Each Other

Set aside thirty minutes to an hour every day to talk to your spouse about your concerns. During these talks, practice using "I" messages (chapter 5). End these conversations by telling your spouse something he or she did that day that you appreciate: "Thanks for going to work to support the family," "I appreciate you dropping Jeffery off at practice," or even, "I noticed you remembered to put the toilet seat down." Don't withdraw from conflicts. It is okay to take a time-out when arguments start to escalate, as long as you specify the length of the time-out and come back to the discussion after you both have cooled off. Being a good communicator involves not only being able to express yourself in a positive manner but also learning how to be a good listener. As your spouse is talking, repeat in your head what you heard your spouse say. Say out loud what you think your spouse said and ask your spouse if this is what he or she meant. Ask your spouse to clarify anything you missed or didn't understand. If you want your spouse to just listen to you vent, tell him or her that you don't want your problem solved, you just need him or her to support you by listening.

Compliment Your Partner and Show Appreciation

Avoid taking your partner for granted by letting him or her know on a frequent and regular basis what you appreciate about him or her. Thank him or her for doing the laundry, taking out the trash, or dressing up to go out with you. Focus on complimenting rather than criticizing. Let him or her know that he or she is special and important to you.

Remember to continue doing romantic things for one another throughout your marriage. Continuing to do little things for each other will help build the love that began when you started dating and will help you avoid taking your spouse for granted. Keeping romance alive does require effort. Without planning and commitment it will soon be relegated to the "when I have some spare time" department. The following exercise will help you continue to strengthen the bond between you and your spouse.

EXERCISE 14: HOW DO I LOVE YOU? LET ME SHOW YOU THE WAYS

As you plan your schedule for the week, write down one or more of the following to do in that week.

- Send your spouse a friendship or love card.

- E-mail or fax your spouse a funny cartoon at work.

- Give your spouse a coupon good for a night of dancing, dinner, a back rub, a picnic in the park, or being his or her slave for a night.

- Do something with your spouse that he or she likes to do but isn't something you really enjoy. (You may find out that you enjoy country line dancing after all.)

- Take up a new activity together that neither one of you has tried before.

- Buy a hot tub. They are great conversation pits because you can't do much in them except relax, talk, and have fun.

- Go for a walk or bike ride together.

- Sit and listen to music together.

- Hold hands while watching TV.

- Go to a comedy club or coffeehouse together.

- Call your spouse every day at work just to let him or her know that you are thinking about him or her.

- Send your spouse a love letter that states very specifically what you love about him or her.

- Rent a room for the night.

- Put sticky notes on your spouse's steering wheel that express love or just read, "Have a great day."

- Fill a picnic basket and take your spouse on a picnic.

- Run a bubble bath for your spouse surrounded by candles, chocolates, and champagne.

- Do a chore your spouse normally does.

- Take your spouse's car to the car wash or fill up the tank with gas.

- Send flowers to your spouse at home or at work.

- Buy and read a book on intimacy.

- Plan, shop for, and cook your spouse's favorite foods.

- Write down three reasons why you married your spouse and put it in his or her lunch or car or on the pillow.

- Buy a romantic song and play it while eating a romantic dinner. Make it "our song."

- Write on separate slips of paper seven things you like about your spouse and have him or her read one out loud every morning over coffee for a week.

- Send your spouse on a romantic treasure hunt. Wrap up several small gifts and hide them throughout the house. Provide a clue as to where you hid the first gift. With the first gift leave a clue to the location of the next gift. Continue the procedure with each gift, and on the final gift give a clue that directs your spouse to the backyard where you're waiting with a picnic basket or to the dining room where you've fixed a romantic dinner.

- Ask your spouse to write down five things he or she would like for you to do this week and then do them.

- Sign up for a class together that your spouse has been talking about wanting to do, such as painting, woodworking, or swing dance.

- Ask your spouse out for a date. Let your spouse know that you had such a wonderful time you want to do this once a week from now until forever.

- In the Personal Notes section at the back of the book, jot down ideas for other romantic things you can do for your spouse. Choose items that are special and out of the ordinary.

Establish a Relationship Separate from Your Family of Origin and from Previous Relationships

This doesn't mean you sever ties with extended family. It means redefining relationships with your and your spouse's parents, siblings, and other relatives. Discuss with your spouse decisions and problems with extended family and previous spouses and decide together how to approach these issues. Talk about how each of you have spent family holidays, birthdays, and Sunday dinners in the past and establish your own traditions for the future. My sister spent Christmas Eve alone with her husband and children each year. They would go to Mass together and Santa would come while they were at church. After the kids went to bed, her husband and she would share a bottle of wine and open their gifts to each other. On Christmas Day they would then travel to visit extended family. This tradition helped them bond as a family and reduced the stress that most families experience during the holidays.

10

Stepparenting

"Some luck lies in not getting what you thought you wanted but getting what you have, which once you've got it you might be smart enough to see is what you would have wanted had you known."

—Garrison Keillor.

KEY POINTS

- Allow your children to have a relationship with their stepparent.
- Develop a positive relationship with your stepchildren.
- Be aware that stepfamilies are different than birth families.
- Do not try to take the place of the other parent.
- Do not start off as the disciplinarian.
- Discuss with your spouse financial issues.
- Do activities together as a family.
- Spend time alone with your stepchildren.
- Praise your stepchildren for their accomplishments.
- Discuss with family members, parents, and children privacy issues and boundaries.
- Discuss with extended family their role with your stepchildren.

As a child, while playing with your Barbie and Ken dolls, you didn't dream about someday being part of a stepfamily. As a young adult, making decisions about career and family, you probably didn't picture yourself trying to convince your own children that they will learn to love your new spouse. Your goals for the future probably didn't include developing a relationship with your spouse's six-, ten-, and thirteen-year-old children. As you matured and you figured out that real women don't look like Barbie, you also discovered that life doesn't always end up the way you planned. You may also discover that with patience, prudence, and persistence, being part of a stepfamily, despite its challenges, can be a rewarding and enriching part of your and your children's lives.

Developing Relationships Between Stepchildren and Stepparents

Just as you can love more than one child without loving your other children less, your children can love both a parent and a stepparent. Do not feel threatened if your children call their stepparent Mom or Dad. The more hostility that exists between the two of you, the more difficult it will be for your children to adjust. Instead of seeing your children's growing affection toward their stepparent as a threat, focus on how being loved by another adult can enhance your children's emotional security.

Thanks to Cinderella and numerous other myths and attitudes throughout history, stepparents have a bad reputation. Even in the modern remake of the story, *Ever After,* Cinderella is viewed as a strong independent character. The stepmother, however, is still portrayed as a selfish vindictive woman who never loves or cares for her stepdaughter and, in the end, is punished for it. Contrary to the fairytale, however, stepparents can add enrichment and quality to their stepchildren's lives. There are very specific things you as a stepparent can do to build a positive relationship with your stepchildren (other than marrying them off to the next available handsome prince or princess).

Do not expect that your stepfamily will be a replica of your pre-divorce family. Stepfamilies have their own special problems and rewards. In an intact family the couple joins together to create and raise children. In a stepfamily, biological ties can polarize families and create animosity between family members. Be aware that family members do not have shared history. Your ways of doing things and your beliefs may be different. Approach these differences with openness, understanding, and respect. Introduce change slowly. You may think it's disgusting that your stepdaughter likes mayonnaise and pickles on her peanut butter sandwich but who knows, if you try it maybe you'll find you'll like it too.

It helps to view your initial role as being a mentor rather than an authority figure. Both you and your stepchildren need time to adjust to this new family. Your stepchildren may still be mourning the loss of their biological family and may view you as the person who keeps their parents from reuniting. It takes time for relationships to grow and to develop decision-making skills as a family.

"When I first married Susan, her son Rick continually reminded me that I wasn't his real father. It really made me mad because I was the one that was taking him to football practice, shooting hoops with him on the driveway, and paying most of the bills. His real dad hardly even bothered to come and see him. At first I would point out to Rick all the things that I did for him that his 'real dad' didn't do. This just made things worse so I tried to just ignore it. Finally, I took Rick out for pizza, just the two of us, and I told him that he was right, that I wasn't his dad because he already had one. (I didn't add, 'even though your real dad is a loser,' even though that's what I thought.) I let him know that the relationship he had with his dad was very special and that no one could ever change that. I told Rick that I could never take his dad's place but that I did care about him. I told him how much I liked playing basketball with him and how proud I was of how much he had improved this year in football. I explained that as one of the adults in the family, I would sometimes tell him what to do and that I understood that sometimes he wouldn't like it. I let him know that I planned on being there for him and that I loved him. After that things got better. Rick would continue to remind me now and then that I wasn't his 'real dad' but that was usually when I reminded him of his curfew or chores. I would respond by saying, 'I know I'm not your dad, but you still have to be home by eleven'" (Jack, stepparent to a thirteen-year-old).

Accept that you will never be your stepchild's "real" mother or father. Instead work on building a unique relationship with your children that can be rewarding for both of you. *Present yourself as the male or female head of the household rather than the mother or father.*

Choose a name for your stepchildren to call you that you are both comfortable with. Children find it awkward to have to figure out what to call their stepparent. They may not feel close enough to you to call you Mom or Dad or worry that their biological parent will be upset if they do. On the other hand, if they have been taught not to address adults by their first name, calling you Bill may seem disrespectful to them. It is important that you sit down with your stepchildren and come up with a name that all of you are comfortable with. Kenny, nine, called his stepmom Mandy. This was a cross between her name, Sandy, and Mom.

Loyalty issues are often very intense in stepfamilies, leading children to experience mixed feelings about their stepparent. "When Mom married Brian, I had a lot of mixed feelings. Part of me was really happy. He treated my mom well and he didn't try to tell me what to do. He was a chemist and helped me with my physics and chemistry homework. He even agreed to help me pay for college. But part of me felt kind of guilty, like I was fraternizing with the enemy" (Marsha, seventeen). Don't be surprised if your stepchildren vacillate between being open and cooperative with you and going out of their way to be nasty. Try to understand their ambivalence and continue to work on building a positive relationship with them. At the same time, support your children's relationship with their birth parent (or adoptive parent). Avoid putting your children's parent down or badmouthing him or her in any way, which will undermine your relationship with your stepchildren. It will put your stepchildren in the position of defending their biological parent against you even if what you say about that person is true.

Instead of trying to make your children perfect, work on perfecting your relationship with them. Do not start off as the disciplinarian. Coming into a new relationship with the attitude of "my way or the highway" will alienate your stepchildren. Your spouse may also react by overprotecting or underdisciplining his or her biological children. First work on building a relationship and getting to know your spouse's approach to discipline. In the beginning, allow your spouse to be the one to discipline the children. This does not mean that you become a doormat. Children need structure. Discuss with your spouse what chores and duties are expected of each family member, what the family rules should be, and what the consequences of breaking these rules are. Chapter 3 will help you set up and follow a set of household rules that both you and your spouse agree upon. Reinforce these rules with all of the children in the household even if they are only there for the day or weekend.

Clarify with your spouse who will make decisions about school placement and medical or legal issues regarding your stepchildren. Find out if you will have legal rights to make any of these decisions. Your stepchildren's other parent will need to be consulted when these decisions are made, so talk to your spouse about what role you will play in these discussions and decisions.

In the Personal Notes section at the back of this book, jot down ideas about what you can do to build your relationship with your stepchildren.

Financial Issues

Work on developing a budget together. "When Katie and I were first married, her son Calvin asked her for his allowance. She gave him ten dollars. Later that evening, while Katie was at the store, he asked me for some money to go to the show. When I told him to use his allowance, he looked at me like I was from another planet and said, 'Yeah, right' as he held out his hand. I gave him the ten but told him we'd have to talk with his mother about what he was expected to use his allowance for" (Jack, stepfather of four). Discuss with your spouse how both of you have approached allowances in the past and how choices about money will be made in the future. Talk about the purpose of allowances (to teach responsibility, learn to make choices, or simply to stop begging Mom for money every day). Some families give their teens a large allowance but expect the children to purchase everything from clothing to school lunches with it. Other families expect the children to give part of their money to charity or save a percentage. I have an agreement with my children that I will match every dollar they put in their college fund.

The following exercise will help you use allowances to motivate your stepchildren to help out with household chores.

EXERCISE 15:   SHOW ME THE MONEY

Step 1: Make a list of all of the chores that both parents think each child is capable of doing.

Step 2: Decide with the other parent what a reasonable allowance should be for each child.

Step 3: List each of your children's names in the first column in the blank chart that follows.

Step 4: At the start of each week or at the family meeting, have your children write in their assigned chores for the week along with the time you expect them to be completed (empty the dishwasher before dinner or mow the lawn on Saturday before noon). Having them write it will help them remember to do it.

Step 5: Discuss with your children what the specific expectations are for each job (doing the dishes means loading the dishwasher, putting away leftover food or condiments, and wiping off the counter and table). If your children are not going to be with you on any of these days, color those days in or write "with Dad/Mom."

Step 6: Post the chart in a visible location. The refrigerator door works well.

Step 7: Each day that your child does his or her chore by the specified time, he or she earns one-seventh of the weekly allowance. That amount is written on the square that lists the chore. If the chore is not done on time, write a zero in the square.

Step 8: With your children, add up the amount they have earned at the end of the week and give it to them.

Step 9: Give your children a bonus for completing their jobs every day that they were with you.

Our Family Chores

Child's Name	Mon	Tues	Wed	Thurs	Fri	Sat	Sun	Total

Below is a sample chore list that my family uses to help clarify chores.

Child's Name	Mon	Tues	Wed	Thurs	Fri	Sat	Sun	Totals
Jessica	Feed cat before breakfast.	Feed cat before breakfast.	Feed cat before breakfast.	Feed cat before breakfast.	Feed cat before breakfast.	Feed cat before breakfast.	Feed cat before breakfast.	Feed cat before breakfast.
	Set table at 4:30.	Set table at 4:30.	Set table at 4:30. Empty trash at 7:30	Set table at 4:30.	Set table at 4:30.	Set table at 4:30.	Set table at 4:30.	Set table at 4:30.
Josh	Give cat fresh water before breakfast.	Give cat fresh water before breakfast.	Give cat fresh water before breakfast.	Give cat fresh water before breakfast.	Give cat fresh water before breakfast.	Give cat fresh water before breakfast.	Give cat fresh water before breakfast.	Give cat fresh water before breakfast.
	Clear table after dinner.	Vacuum. Clear table after dinner.	Clear table after dinner.	Clear table after dinner.	Clear table after dinner.	Clear table after dinner.	Clear table after dinner.	Clear table after dinner.

Variations:

- If your children have trouble remembering to do their jobs, spend time having them think of ways that will help them remember, such as writing themselves a note or doing the job before the TV gets turned on or before they go out to play. You can give them a daily bonus if they do their jobs without having to be reminded.

- If your child wants extra money, add optional jobs he or she can do to earn more.

- You can also split the allowance and give half of it for doing chores and half of it for following the family rules.

Developing Your Parenting Skills

The fact that you're reading this book demonstrates your commitment to your children. Additional support can be obtained by taking a parenting class for stepparents with your spouse. These classes help build your confidence as a parent and facilitate cooperation and communication with your spouse and stepchildren. Check with your local school, church, or family service agency to locate classes available in your neighborhood. Meanwhile, here are some guidelines and tips you can begin implementing right now.

Think Up New Activities to Do Together as a Family

"When I first married Kendra it seemed that her kids compared everything I did to their dad. I didn't scramble eggs the way their dad did. I didn't play Ping-Pong the way their dad played. I didn't even cut the grass the way their dad did. So I decided to do something that they had never done with their dad. I asked my wife if there was anything that they had not done that she thought the kids would enjoy. One of her ideas was downhill skiing. I had never done it either but it sounded like fun. I booked a weekend, skis, and lessons at a resort a friend recommended that focuses on family skiing. Despite my looking like a giant snowman by the end of the day, we had a blast. At the end of the weekend the kids wanted to know when we were going again and they didn't mention their dad one time" (George, stepfather of three).

Create new family traditions and do things together to build family cohesion. Use the following exercise to build family cohesion by making a family mobile together. This idea comes from *The Family Book of People Projects,* by Ray and Jean Noll.

EXERCISE 16: OUR NEW FAMILY

Materials

Scissors, glue, markers or crayons, string, construction paper

Photographs of each member of the household (optional)

Empty round container such as a cottage cheese, yogurt, or margarine tub

Step 1: Using your empty container, have your children draw several circles on the construction paper. You will need one circle for each family member.

Step 2: In each of the circles, you or your children draw a picture of each household member. You can also cut out photographs of each household member and glue them on the circles instead of drawing them.

Step 3: Cut out the circles.

Step 4: Cut strings for each circle that are approximately five to thirteen inches. Each string should be a different length.

Step 5: Tie a piece of string to each circle.

Step 6: On a sheet of construction paper draw a rectangle eleven by two inches and cut it out.

Step 7: Glue or staple the ends of the rectangle together to form a circle.

Step 8: Tie the other end of each string from step 5 to the bottom of the circle.

Step 9: Tie three foot-long strings to the top of this circle.

Step 10: Hang the mobile in a prominent place.

Spend Time Alone with Your Stepchildren

Do a project or develop a hobby with your stepchildren such as building a model plane or putting a jigsaw puzzle together. Go to a ball game or out to lunch together. Use the list from chapter 2, What I Like to Do with My Mom/Dad, for some ideas on things that you can do together. In the Personal Notes section at the back of this book, write down ideas for new traditions you can start in your family, and ideas for spending time alone with your stepchildren.

Praise Your Stepchildren for Their Accomplishments

Acknowledging your stepchildren's accomplishments will help build your relationship with them as well as help build their self-esteem. Matthew McKay and Patrick Fanning, in *Self-Esteem,* recommend that for praise to be effective in enhancing self-esteem, it must include three things:

1. A description of the behavior. "I noticed you remembered to feed the dog this morning without having to be reminded." Describe the behavior without using the words "good" or "bad." Describing behavior (what happened, what you saw or heard) lets your children know how their behavior affects others. It also helps to point out to your stepchildren the effect positive behavior has on how people feel about themselves. Instead of saying, "You're so smart," say, "You must be so proud of getting all of your spelling words right on your test this week!"

2. Your reaction to the behavior. Share your feelings about what your stepchildren did and why you felt that way. "I was impressed by the courage it must have taken to tell your friend you would not ride in his car if he was drinking."

3. Acknowledgement of the child's feelings. Validate your children's efforts and their feelings. This will help your stepchildren know that you listen to them and care about their feelings. "I realize you were upset about having to leave the party before your friend Monica did, and I appreciate you getting home on time."

Use all three parts when praising your stepchildren:

"You ran really hard and put a hundred percent into that race (Description). I know you were disappointed at not winning (Acknowledgment). I admire how hard your trained for that race and I loved watching you pass those two boys who were older than you (Reaction).

"The pencil holder you made me is beautiful. I especially like the purple and blue flowers (Description). It means a lot that you made it just for me (Reaction). I can tell you put a lot of time and effort into it (Acknowledgment). I'm going to put it on my desk at work so that everyone there can see it."

Using the spaces below, write three things that your stepchildren have done that met with your approval.

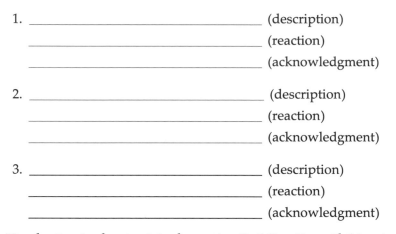

1. _____ (description)
   _____ (reaction)
   _____ (acknowledgment)

2. _____ (description)
   _____ (reaction)
   _____ (acknowledgment)

3. _____ (description)
   _____ (reaction)
   _____ (acknowledgment)

Use the tips in chapter 6, in the section Building Your Children's Self-Esteem," for further assistance.

The Role of an Extended Family

As I was writing this book, I discovered that my spell check doesn't recognize the words "stepgrandparent," "stepuncle," or "stepaunt." Your parents or siblings may be just as confused about what their role with your stepchildren should be. Talk to them about what kind of relationship they expect to have with your stepchildren. Share with them what your hopes are as well. If they want to have a relationship with your stepchildren, advise them to go slow. Remember that, initially, they are strangers and it will take time to build a relationship. If they are open to it and both parents agree, they can spoil their new relatives and do all of the activities with them that they do with their other grandchildren or nieces and nephews. Keep in mind that your biological children may be jealous of having to share Aunt Eileen or Grandma Bredow. Extended family should continue rituals with your children that have already been established. Finally, your parents should consult with their attorney before changing their will to include stepgrandchildren.

Your Children's Relationship with Their Stepsiblings

Blending two families together is not as easy as pie but it is like baking one. When you bake, you blend ingredients to make an end product that is nothing like any of the original ingredients. When you put two different families together, you get challenges and rewards that none of you experienced in your predivorce families. Children who do not have biological ties and have not been raised together will relate differently to each other than siblings raised together from birth. Anticipate some territorial disputes and jealousy over both you and your new spouse sharing your love and attention with other children. If you are remaining in your home, your children may feel invaded. If you are moving into your spouse's home, your children will feel like strangers in a new land. The same is true for your spouse's children.

If you want to keep your pie from spilling all over the oven, put a baking sheet underneath it before you put it in to cook. If you are trying to prevent hurt and anger from spilling over onto your family, talk to all of the children before you marry someone who has children of his or her own. Give them details about where everyone will be sleeping and when the children will be in and out of the home. Discuss with family members, parents, and children privacy issues and boundaries such as not going in each other's rooms without that person's permission or walking around the house in a towel. This is especially true if the stepsiblings are adolescents or preadolescents of different sexes.

Give each child a specific space of his or her own and clarify which items are private, such as the autographed baseball mitt, saxophone, or ballet shoes. Establish rules about borrowing each other's things and which items are for the use of the entire family. For example, "All family members can use the TV, Nintendo set, and the computer. If you want to use anyone's clothing, personal items, and other toys, you must ask that person first." Help each child find a quiet place to be alone. I grew up in a family of nine, and after church each

Sunday I would sit by myself in the car just so I could have a few minutes of peace and quiet. Children and adults need quiet time and a place to call their own.

Encourage your children and stepchildren to talk to each other. They may also have been through divorce and understand what it feels like. Reading children's stories about stepfamilies, talking to them about how they are feeling, and continuing to spend time alone with them can help your children and your stepchildren accept each other. Let your children know that there will always be a special place in your heart for them and that you will continue to love them.

Despite its challenges, stepparenting can be a rich and rewarding experience. With time, patience, and persistence, stepparents can form meaningful relationships with their stepchildren. Stepparents can help build their stepchildren's self-esteem and provide them with a strong basis for developing into well-adjusted and functioning adults. Remember that blended families, like pies, take time to cool before you can enjoy them. You may have to make adjustments and modify your beliefs about how things should be done. You will discover, however, that the final product is worth the time and effort.

11

Taking Care of Yourself

KEY POINTS

- Take care of yourself so that you can take care of your children.
- Work on reducing your stress.
- Slow down and enjoy life.
- Work on building your self-esteem.
- Do daily affirmations.
- Set realistic goals for the future.
- Choose friends who are positive.
- Spend time with other adults.

If you treat your friends the way you treat yourself, will you have any friends? If you are going to be able to help your children through the divorce, you must take care of yourself. This is often the hardest part for parents. You may feel that you have torn your children's lives apart and don't deserve to focus on your own needs. However, if you are depressed, overstressed, fatigued, or worried about finances, you will tend to be an irritable and resentful parent. Just as you can't keep driving a car without stopping for gas, you can't keep giving to your children without stopping to refuel emotionally. Neglecting your body, being stressed out, and experiencing low self-esteem can also increase your chances of getting sick, which will interfere with your ability to take care of your children. This chapter will assist you in taking care of your physical and emotional needs, which will put you in a much better position to help your children.

Reducing Your Stress

Some stress in your life is normal—it is what provides challenge and opportunity to you. Often, however, particularly during a divorce, we have too much stress. When we experience dramatic changes in our life, our stress level dramatically increases, which can affect our emotional and physical well-being. It can decrease our ability to fight infection and make us less effective at school, home, and work. We need to learn to recognize that we are under stress and do something about it.

Identify What is Causing You Stress, and When

The first step in eliminating a problem is to identify it. Recognize what causes you stress. Take an inventory of experiences that cause you stress and ask yourself the following questions:

What in my environment is causing me stress?

What physical changes are increasing my stress?

Have I been sick?

Am I getting enough sleep?

Am I eating a balanced diet and exercising?

Has there been a recent change in my routine?

Has there been a change in my relationships with family or friends?

Am I able to pay my bills?

Are there changes at work?

Is my negative thinking causing me stress?

Identifying when you are feeling stressed is a skill that must be learned. Paying attention to your feelings, thoughts, and physical changes in your body will assist you in recognizing that you are feeling stressed out. Are you feeling tense, strained, anxious, agitated, apprehensive, distressed, panicky, afraid, frustrated, irritable, testy, cranky, worried, troubled, or bothered? Those feelings can be signs of stress. You can recognize physical signs of stress by paying attention to what is happening in your body. Clammy palms, clenched teeth, tight muscles, rigid body posture, or knots in your stomach are all physical signs of stress. Increase in pulse or heart rate, sweating, and rapid breathing and flushed face not associated with intense physical activity can also be physical clues that you are under stress.

Once you have identified the source and symptoms of your stress, you can take short- and long-term measures to reduce it. The following exercise will give you an immediate, short-term activity to help in reducing your stress.

EXERCISE 17: STRESS STOPPER

Step 1: Whenever you feel stressed, take a five- to ten-minute break from what you are doing by going into a room by yourself, such as your bedroom or office or even a rest room, and shutting the door.

Step 2: Get in a comfortable position, either lying flat on your back or sitting in a chair.

Step 3: If you are in a chair, place your feet flat on the floor, legs uncrossed.

Step 4: Take slow deep breaths. Inhale through your nose and out through your mouth.

Step 5: Slowly count forward and backward from ten, inhaling as you say each number. Do this until you feel your muscles relax.

Ten Healthy Habits to Handle Stress

To help prevent stress and make you more able to cope with it on a longer-term basis when it does arise, adhere to the guidelines that follow. Practice them everyday until they have become positive habits. Encouraging your children to follow these guidelines with you will assist them in coping with stress as well.

1. Eat nutritionally.

    Take care of your body and appreciate that it has brought you this far. Limit your intake of alcohol, caffeine, sugar, and fat. Eat a balanced diet and don't skip breakfast. Eat lots of fruits, vegetables, and complex carbohydrates. Don't focus on dieting. In general, if you eat a balanced diet 95 percent of the time, you can eat whatever you want 5 percent of the time.

2. Exercise.

    Exercise is a healthy way of discharging anxiety and tension. Use part of your lunch hour to take a walk. Invite a friend to exercise with you. Find an activity that you enjoy: sign up for a kickboxing class or take your children swimming every Tuesday night. Schedule exercise in your planner a minimum of twenty minutes, three times a week.

3. Get enough sleep.

More and more, Americans are realizing how important sleep is to our emotional and physical well-being. The media is flooding us with research and statistics about how much we need a good night's sleep. Often during a divorce we don't get enough sleep, which diminishes our ability to cope. Feeling rested will help you deal calmly with children, colleagues, and everyday problems that arise. The following exercise can help you condition yourself to fall asleep.

EXERCISE 18: OH WHAT GLORIOUS SLEEP

The following suggestions will be most effective if you follow all of them, preferably for two to three weeks. If you do not notice any results after two to three weeks, consult with your physician.

1. Avoid all caffeine (chocolate, tea, coffee, and many soft drinks) three to five hours before bedtime.

2. Avoid alcohol and sleeping pills. According to experts at St. John Hospital Sleep Disorder Center, alcohol and sleeping pills can create drug dependency for sleep and make sleep more fragmented and more easily disrupted.

3. Stop smoking. Research shows that smoking one pack of cigarettes a day reduces sleeping almost a half hour per night.

4. Sleep in a dark, quiet, comfortable space.

5. Avoid naps. Naps tend to interfere with the sleep-wake cycle and may contribute to insomnia.

6. Avoid computer work or TV prior to bedtime, because their screens can stimulate brain activity.

7. Practice wind-down activities before bedtime. Light reading or listening to relaxing music may help. Listening to natural-sound tapes, such as of waves or birds, also helps.

8. Don't do anything in bed except sleep; don't eat or watch TV. You are trying to program your mind and body to sleep when you lay down in bed.

9. Experiment with your bedroom's temperature. Avoid temperatures above seventy-five degrees and below sixty-three degrees.

10. Regular daily exercise (a half hour per day) can deepen sleep. Do not, however, exercise just prior to bedtime. This can stimulate your body rather than relax it.

11. Go to bed and wake up at the same time every day. This will help your body follow a sleep-wake cycle. This cycle is kind of like a built-in clock that tells your mind and body when they're supposed to be sleeping and when they're supposed to be awake.

12. Try to adhere to this same schedule on the weekends. If you stay up later than usual on Friday night, try to get up at your usual time Saturday morning and then take a short (half hour) nap Saturday afternoon to combat feeling groggy.

13. If you are in the habit of waking up to go to the bathroom during the night, restrict fluids two hours before bedtime.

14. Have regular mealtimes. Make breakfast and lunch your large meals. Eat a light supper several hours before bedtime. Don't go to bed hungry. A light snack, particularly if it has calcium in it, such as milk, yogurt, or cheese, may help. If you wake up during the night, do not eat. Remember, you are conditioning yourself to sleep at night, not eat.

15. If noise wakes you up at night, try a white-noise machine.

16. Use relaxation exercises such as the ones in this chapter to help you fall asleep. There are also numerous relaxation tapes that can walk you through these steps.

17. If you still cannot fall back asleep after trying step 16, get out of bed to avoid further frustration. Try drinking a warm caffeine-free beverage. Read or listen to some music or engage in another relaxing activity. When you feel tired, go back to bed.

18. If you lay awake mulling over things you need to do or worrying about something you did, keep a pad of paper near your bed. Write down what you're thinking about and tell yourself you will deal with it tomorrow. Schedule time every day to go over this list. This helps you program yourself to deal with problems during the day and not when

you're trying to sleep. In the Personal Notes section at the back of this book, write down peaceful calming things and places you can think about at bedtime to help you sleep.

---

4. Take time for yourself every day.

Take a yoga class, read your favorite magazine, or take a hot bath. Do daily relaxation exercises or listen to a relaxation tape of waves or whales. (Most music and bookstores carry a selection of such tapes.) The following exercise will also help you feel relaxed and more able to cope throughout the day.

EXERCISE 19: RELAXATION

Step 1: In your planner, schedule thirty minutes of relaxation several times a week.

Step 2. Sit or lie down in a darkened room.

Step 3. Breathe deeply. Take slow deep breaths. Inhale through your nose and out through your mouth.

Step 4: Start with your right foot. Tighten your toes, the ball, and the heel of your foot.

Step 5: Hold it for a few seconds and release.

Step 6: Feel the difference between the foot when it is tense and when it's relaxed.

Step 7: Now tense your left foot. Tighten your toes, the ball, and the heel of your foot.

Step 8: Hold it for a few seconds and release.

Step 9: Follow steps 4–8 with your calf muscles.

Step 10: Move on to your thighs. Remember to keep breathing deeply.

Step 11: Move up your body, tensing and relaxing one muscle group at a time. Do your pelvis, your stomach, your chest, your hands, your arms, your shoulders and back, your neck, your jaw, your nose and eyes, and then your forehead and scalp.

Step 12: Check each part of your body. If you feel any tension in that area, repeat steps 4–8 with each part of your body that is still tense.

Step 13: Picture yourself in a quiet setting: walking in a cool forest, fishing on a lake, or lying on an ocean beach. Choose one that would create a relaxed feeling for you.

Step 14: Spend about ten minutes or longer imagining what you would see, hear, smell, feel, and taste if you were actually in that quiet setting right now. Hear the birds, feel the breeze, smell the pine trees.

Step 15: Keep breathing deeply and slowly.

Step 16: Tell yourself that you will carry this relaxed feeling with you throughout the day and that you can handle whatever life brings to you.

Step 17: When you are ready, refocus (in your mind) on the room you are in. Picture the furniture and wall color.

Step 18: Open your eyes.

Step 19: Notice that even after you open your eyes, you still feel relaxed.

---

5. Manage your time.

"When I got home from work at six, I immediately started cooking dinner. This seemed to be the most urgent thing to do. It was so frustrating. My kids would be putting school notes and papers in my face, asking me for money or supplies for some school project or help with their homework. I was so frazzled. Finally, I realized that what was important to me and what my children needed as soon as I got home was to spend some time with each other. Now when I get home, I give them a piece of fruit or carrot sticks and sit down with each one of them for fifteen minutes before I start dinner. Since they don't have to act up or interrupt to get my attention, it takes me less time to cook and we actually eat at about the same time we did when I was so stressed out. Sometimes I make dinner a family project so that I can be with them and still get dinner on the table" (Kelly, mother of three). We spend most of our time doing what is urgent rather than what is important. Plan your time and set short- and long-term goals. Take an inventory of what is important and what you can realistically accomplish. Delegate when you can and acknowledge yourself for the things you do accomplish.

6. Get control of your finances.

One of the main worries for divorced adults is money. The reality is that it costs more to maintain two households. To reduce your worry, take an inventory of all your household and personal expenses and income sources. There are numerous books and software programs that offer household budgeting assistance. Once you have determined what you spend money on, set financial goals for your family and set up a budget for future expenditures. You will discover that "budget" doesn't have to be a bad word; it can be a way to help you gain control and achieve financial independence.

7. Take vacations.

Getting away, even for a few days, can help you relax and renew yourself. A change of scenery, away from home and work, can assist you in gaining a new perspective. Vacations also give parents and children a chance to bond and spend time together. My family still laughs about the family vacations we took where it rained for days and we were stuck playing marathon Monopoly games together.

8. Start a new hobby.

Getting involved in an activity strictly for pleasure can be very relaxing. Building a model or painting a sweatshirt can help you feel that you are talented and give you an opportunity to take time out from your hectic schedule. For me, working in my garden in the spring and watching what I have planted grow gives me a sense of peace that is absent at other, busier times of my life. Get your children involved in hobbies as well, to help them relax and take pride in what they have created.

9. Get organized.

Unfinished projects and clutter increase our stress. Organize your closets and fix or throw out things you've been meaning to fix for months. Give away clothes you haven't worn for a year.

Make a daily written list of what you intend to do each day. As you accomplish things on the list, check them off and praise yourself for accomplishing each task. Don't procrastinate. Putting things off increases your guilt and lowers your productivity.

"When I packed up that last box of Jeremy's (my ex-husband's) stuff and sent it to him, it felt like a huge weight was lifted off my shoulders. It may seem kind of silly, but throwing away his toothbrush was my way of declaring that he wasn't coming back" (Marty, mother of five). Help give yourself a sense of closure on your marriage by sorting and giving the other parent his or her personal items or clothes that are still in the closets or stored in the basement.

10. Stop and smell the roses.

Take time to enjoy life and play with your children. Enjoy the hot water when you're taking a shower rather than using it as time to plan your day. Taste the food you eat, breathe in the fresh air as you walk, and sit down to pet your dog or cat. When you're driving in the car, look at the scenery or listen to a good book on tape rather than yell at incompetent drivers. Listed below are twenty recommendations to help you slow down and ease up. They come from Richard Carlson's *Don't Sweat the Small Stuff . . . and It's All Small Stuff*. I have modified the author's ideas to assist divorced families.

Accept that you, your children, and the other parent are all imperfect.

Tell yourself that when you die, your "in basket" won't be empty.

Let the other parent and your children be right.

Say to yourself, "Life is not an emergency."

Say thanks to someone every day.

Focus on being a good listener.

Ask yourself, "Will this matter a year from now?"

First, seek to understand.

Identify your most stubborn positions and try to soften them.

Be flexible when your plans change.

Avoid battles and choose conflicts wisely.

Tell everyone in your family (today) how much you love them.

Take a moment every day to identify what about your life is good.

Understand that you and your former partner may have separate realities.

Take three deep breaths before you say something to your former partner.

Choose being generous over being right.

Focus on one thing at a time.

Cut yourself, your children, and their other parent some slack.

Just because someone throws you the ball doesn't mean you have to catch it.

Become comfortable with not knowing.

In the Personal Notes section at the back of this book, write down a few things you can do *this week* to reduce your stress.

Building Your Self-Esteem

Someone once said, "You might as well love yourself because you're going to take yourself everywhere you go." How we judge ourselves affects how we get along with others, what kinds of friends we choose, who we marry, our success at work, and even the type of parent we are. Our self-esteem affects how we think, what we feel, and which actions we take. Self-esteem is the feeling you have about yourself. It is your perception of your self-worth. When going through a divorce, you may not feel capable and lovable. You may think of yourself as a failure, which lowers your self-esteem. It is crucial that you focus on rebuilding it. The following exercise will help you build your self-esteem through daily affirmations. Many of these affirmations were modified suggestions made by self-esteem expert Jack Canfield.

EXERCISE 20:
I WILL SURVIVE: BUILDING SELF-ESTEEM THROUGH DAILY AFFIRMATIONS

Step 1: Tell your family why you are doing this exercise and invite them to participate.

Step 2: Every morning choose one affirmation from the list below.

Step 3: Write your name in the blank.

Step 4: Copy the statement on a three-by-five card.

Step 5: Post the card in a spot where you will see it throughout the day, for example, your bathroom mirror, the refrigerator, or above the kitchen sink.

Step 6: Read the card out loud several times a day.

Step 7: When you have a negative thought about yourself, replace it with one of the affirmations that you have practiced.

Step 8: When others criticize you, use the feedback to make positive changes and identify something that you have done right.

I _____ like myself.

I _____ am lovable.

I _____ determine my future.

I _____ accept compliments because I deserve them.

I _____ see every problem as an opportunity.

I _____ am exceptional.

I _____ take care of myself.

I _____ do the best I can with the skills, knowledge, and experience I have.

I _____ accept myself just as I am.

I _____ like myself and I like others.

I _____ am liked and loved by others.

I _____ deserve to be treated with respect and dignity.

I _____ trust my own intuition.

I _____ can choose what I want and need without having to justify it to anyone else.

I _____ believe that life is good.

I _____ have fun in my life.

I _____ have many talents.

I _____ have much to offer others.

I _____ love myself unconditionally.

I _____ feel much peace and tranquillity.

I _____ take responsibility for my own happiness.

I _____ take responsibility for the choices I make.

I _____ am enough.

I _____ am smart.

I _____ am satisfied with my life.

I _____ accept who I am, just the way I am.

I _____ am exactly who I need to be.

I _____ am super.

I _____ have integrity.

I _____ forgive myself for the mistakes I make.

I _____ learn from my mistakes.

I _____ am wise.

I _____ am an important person.

_____ 's feelings are just as important as other people's feelings.

I _____ feel calm and relaxed.

I _____ am beautiful.

I _____ love and appreciate my body.

I _____ take responsibility for my life.

I _____ love life.

I _____ enjoy life.

I _____ feel calm and relaxed.

I _____ like who I am.

I _____ am proud of what I have accomplished.

I _____ deserve credit for what I have accomplished.

I _____ am clever.

I _____ let go of what I cannot change.

I _____ deserve respect.

I _____ am terrific.

I _____ am honest with myself.

I _____ seek to understand more about myself.

It is not what happens, it is how I _____ respond to what happens that determines the quality of my life.

I _____ take action toward accomplishing my goals.

I _____ allow others to love and support me.

I _____ support and love myself.

I _____ surround myself with positive, loving, and supportive people.

I _____ empower others.

I _____ am empowered by others.

I _____ think and act based on what I believe to be right.

I _____ start each day with hope and joy.

I _____ encourage others to be the best they can be.

I _____ am open to new experiences and opportunities.

I _____ face problems calmly.

I _____ have integrity.

I _____ do not let fear stop me from doing what I need to do to be happy.

I _____ will succeed.

I _____ have the right to say no to the things that will not help me reach my goals.

I _____ ask for help when I need it.

I _____ grow stronger every day.

I _____ get results.

I _____ expect things to work out for the best.

I _____ finish what I start.

I _____ use criticism to assist me in doing what it takes to achieve my goals.

I _____ set goals and do what it takes to reach my goals.

I _____ appreciate what I have.

I _____ am a worthwhile person.

I _____ have a balanced life.

I _____ take risks when I need to.

I _____ make a difference.

I _____ reward myself for what I accomplish.

I _____ am open to feedback.

I _____ easily change my behavior when it keeps me from reaching my goals.

I _____ grow happier each day.

I _____ have the courage it takes to accomplish my goals.

I _____ am a responsible person.

I _____ am accomplishing great things.

I _____ look fabulous.

I _____ am getting to where I want to go.

I _____ am special.

I _____ have imaginative ideas.

I _____ am creative.

I _____ do great work.

I _____ am a champion.

I _____ am fantastic.

I _____ am my own best friend.

I _____ treat myself with respect.

I _____ nurture and take care of myself.

I _____ am wonderful.

I _____ can do it.

I _____ am delightful.

I _____ will survive.

Do Daily Mirror Work

Before you go to bed at night, look in the mirror and tell yourself something specific that you accomplished that day. If it's been a difficult day for you, you may say something like, "I got out of bed," or " I remembered to feed the dog." It doesn't have to be something major, but it does have to be positive. In the Personal Notes section at the back of this book, write down something you have accomplished today. If nothing else, you can write, "I read some pages in a self-help book about helping my children cope with divorce."

Set Goals for the Future

> *"One day Alice came to a fork in the road and saw a Cheshire cat in a tree.*
> *'Which road do I take?' she asked.*
> *'Where do you want to go?' was his response.*
> *'I don't know,' Alice answered.*
> *'Then,' said the cat, 'it doesn't matter.'"*
>
> —Lewis Carroll

It's tough to get where you're going if you don't know where that is. Setting goals for yourself, writing them down, and imagining yourself accomplishing these goals will help motivate you to accomplish them. Make sure your goals are specific, realistic, and obtainable. Start off with setting daily goals. For example, "Today I'm going to send out five resumes, give my children five hugs, or not yell at _____ when he or she calls." After you have achieved success at reaching short-term goals think about what your long-term goals are, for example, going back to school, writing a book, or becoming a teacher. Keep in mind what Jane Wagner once said: "All my life I wanted to be someone; I guess I should have been more specific."

Choose Friends Who Are Positive

"If you want to be a happy, positive, enthusiastic person, stay with happy, positive, enthusiastic people. If you want to catch the flu stay with people who have it. It's all contagious."

—Dr. H. Paul Jacobie

Hang out with people who are positive. Spend time with friends who will help boost your self-esteem and who are not critical. Be with people who will support you in being the best that you can be. Do not isolate yourself from family and friends who are supportive. Ask a friend for a hug; you need physical affection.

Spend Time with Other Adults

Your children cannot take the place of your former partner. Although it is good for you and your children to spend time together, make sure that you are not expecting your children to fill an adult friendship role. Your children are not adults and need to grow and develop at a normal rate. I've often thought of parenting as a balancing act. Balance your family's need to comfort each other with your children's need to individuate. You need to spend time with other adults, so ask a friend or relative to meet you for lunch or take an aerobics class together. Join a bowling or tennis league. Take a ceramics, model railroad, or cooking class. Before you join a club, ask what percentage of the participants are single. Being the only single person in a club full of couples can reinforce your feelings of isolation. A lot of religious organizations have single's clubs or activities. Parents Without Partners is a national organization that holds meetings for single people with children. They host many fun events that provide opportunities for you and your children to meet other single adults and their children.

Taking care of yourself is an essential ingredient in your own and your children's recovery. You cannot expect to be a good parent and emotionally available to your children unless you take care of your own needs. Do what it takes to help yourself so that you can help your children.

12

Confronting and Coping with Your Feelings

"When one door of happiness closes
another one opens.
But often we look so long at the closed door
that we do not see the one that has opened for us.

We must all find these open doors,
and if we believe in ourselves,
we will find them and make ourselves
and our lives as beautiful as God intended."

—Helen Keller

Key Points

- Work on your recovery and grief.
- Feelings of anger, sadness, fear, and guilt are normal.
- Replace your negative thinking with positive self-talk.
- Join a support group or get into therapy to help you cope with painful feelings.

"When Ben left, I spent most of the day just sitting at the kitchen table in my robe, smoking cigarette after cigarette. I didn't feel like doing anything or talking to anyone. It's a good thing I was off work for the summer because I don't know if I would have even bothered going in. One evening I overheard my daughter Stephanie talking to a friend on the phone. She was telling her how she felt like she'd lost both of her parents and she didn't know what to do to help me. It felt like someone had kicked me in the stomach. Not only had I completely upset her life by screwing up my marriage, now my daughter was worrying about how to take care of me! I got up out of that chair and went into her room. We talked and cried for a long time. She told me how much she missed me. After that I started getting dressed each morning, even though I still didn't feel like it. I'd make breakfast for the two of us and sit down and eat it with her. I'd force myself to do little things like taking a shower, watering the plants, or doing the dishes. I found that each time I did something, it felt better. I started swimming every day and finally agreed to go to lunch with my neighbor once a week (she'd been trying to get me to go for two months). It took time and I still have days when I don't feel like getting out of bed, but I put one foot at a time on the floor, get out of bed, and get dressed. Just the act of doing something helps the feeling of hopelessness go away" (Jeanette, mother of a fifteen-year-old daughter).

One of the most difficult yet most important tasks for divorcing parents is dealing with the roller coaster of feelings. Anger, sadness, relief, guilt, jealousy, rage, embarrassment, fear, and confusion will ebb and flow like a tidal wave. At times it will seem impossible to put aside these feelings and focus on what your children need. You may at times feel so engulfed by painful feelings that you cannot function as a parent and fear that you will drown in your anger and depression. But the roller coaster eventually slows down and the storm passes. With time and work, the pain will ebb and you will begin to live again.

The Seven Psychological Tasks of Divorce

Judith Wallerstein identifies seven psychological tasks that adults going through divorce need to accomplish in rebuilding their lives. Although each of these tasks may appear simple in written form, they are not easy. Each task can feel overwhelmingly painful and at times impossible. Get support from friends and family when you need it to help you accomplish each one.

1: Ending the Marriage

The way each couple separates will impact the relationship between all family members throughout the years that follow. Work through your emotional commitment to the marriage (love and hate) and move toward indifference, then mutual respect. You may have reunification fantasies. If you have not accepted that the divorce is final, you may be communicating this in subtle ways to your children. If you are having difficulty accepting that the divorce is final or communicating in a nonjudgmental manner, you may need to discuss your feelings with a supportive listener or professional therapist. Therapy can provide you with a neutral listener who can support you through the emotional roller coaster you may experience. Although it may be very difficult, ending the marriage demands that adults negotiate financial and parenting issues. The reality of unpaid bills and children who need to be fed, sent to school, and otherwise be taken care of demands that you acknowledge that the marriage is over and your life has changed.

2: Mourning the Loss

Acknowledge the loss and mourn the hopes and dreams that will never come to fruition. You need to cry. Through mourning you can gain perspective on what you lost and move on. Even if you don't feel a loss for the person you married, you need to mourn the loss of the symbolic meaning of marriage for you. Many couples keep the relationship going through ongoing court battles. They choose a negative connection rather than no connection. Mourn the loss and move on. (Chapter 6 discusses the stages of grief that you and your children may experience as you go through the divorce process.)

3: Reclaiming Oneself

Reclaiming oneself involves establishing a new identity. A large if not major part of your identity throughout your marriage had been derived from being a wife or husband. This can be a painful process of self-discovery. It may involve moving to a new house, developing new hobbies and interests, developing a career, and discovering new friendships. If you are struggling to find your identity as a single person, reach back to the years before you were married. Work on ridding yourself of the negative inner voice of your former spouse that is critical, demeaning, or demanding. Develop your self-esteem by setting new goals and accomplishing them. In the Personal Notes section at the back of this book, write down something you have dreamed of doing but never did. Picture yourself doing that thing.

4: Resolving or Containing Passions

Identify, accept, and deal with your feelings. If you are the parent that wants the divorce you will feel guilty about hurting your spouse and your children. If you are the one being left you may feel angry, betrayed, and abandoned. Some common feelings you will probably experience as you go through the process of divorce are:

Anger

"I hated her now with a hatred more fatal than indifference because it was the other side of love."

—J. August Strindberg

"After the divorce, my ex started coming to all of Kendra's basketball games and track meets. When we were married, I used to beg him to come but he was always too busy. When I see him sitting there rooting for her, pretending to be the perfect father, it makes me so angry. Why didn't he go to any of her games when we were married? If he had spent that much time with the family when we were married, we might still be together. But when I see the smile on Kendra's face when she sees him there, I try saying to myself, 'Better late than never.' It helps to focus on her happiness rather than my disappointment" (Yvonne, mother of four).

It is normal to have intense feelings of anger during a divorce. You may feel betrayed and abandoned and be angry about broken spiritual and emotional promises. How you express this anger, however, will affect your children. You may feel that you want to punish the other parent and hurt him or her the way you have been hurt. Although these feelings are normal, be very careful not to use your children to get back at "the ex." Deal with your feelings toward the other parent separate from your children. If you are angry with the other parent, talk to friends about your anger when your children cannot hear what you are saying. Try to do this when your children are out of the house. If this isn't feasible, go in your room, shut the door, and turn some background music on so that your children don't hear what you are saying. Ask friends if they mind listening to you vent for a while. Say what you need to say and then let go of the anger. Afterward do some deep breathing to help you relax and refocus. Another way of expressing emotions is by writing letters that you may then decide to mail or tear up. Say whatever you need to say in the letter. If you need to swear and call names, put it in the letter. Writing these letters is for your benefit alone. Do not share these letters with your children. If you do plan on mailing any of these letters, wait a few days, reread the letter, and then rewrite the letter specifying what you want changed. Edit out the name-calling and swear words and focus on the issue that you are trying to resolve. "Whenever my ex-wife did something really stupid, I'd write her a letter, telling her exactly how I felt. After I'd said everything I needed to say, I'd burn the letter. It helped get it off my chest without blowing up in front of the kids" (Jack, father of two). In the Personal Notes section at the back of this book, write down three healthy things you can do when you are angry.

Fear

"I was terrified when Janice left. I didn't have a clue about what to do with three girls. How was I going to run my business, get them to daycare, help them with homework, and make sure they were fed all by myself? The first time my daughter Nancy asked me to pick up tampons at the store, I just looked at her like, 'You've got to be kidding'" (Tom, father of three). Divorce means change and change can be very frightening. Initially, you wonder if you will be able to financially support yourself, if you'll know what to do when your three-year-old wakes up in the middle of the night screaming for his mother, or what to do when the lights go out and the hot water heater breaks down. Say to yourself, "Most of what I worried about last month never happened." Use positive self-talk (discussed later in this chapter) to change negative and critical thinking.

Sadness

"The first time Sarah went to stay with her dad, I thought I was going to die. I laid in Sarah's bed and cried for hours. It may sound really weird but I would hold her favorite sweater up to my face and smell it. I missed her so much" (Karen, mother of a two-year-old). Deal with your feelings of loss that come with shared parenting. Not getting a butterfly kiss at bedtime every night from your daughter or a kiss good-bye every morning as your son leaves for school can be very painful. Try to view the changes that occur as different rather than bad and create new rituals and ways of communicating to your children that you love them. Make use of the time you have with your children. Many divorced parents spend more quality time with their children after the divorce because they no longer take the time they have with them for granted. Single parents also discover that parenting roles become less rigid. Fathers learn how to braid hair and mothers learn how to repair bicycle chains.

Guilt

The six-letter word for guilt is "parent," and divorced parents bring to guilt a whole new dimension. You feel guilty that you're breaking up the family, that your children are hurt, that finances are tight, or that you aren't with your children as much. Be very careful not to make decisions regarding your parenting based on guilt. Parents who overbuy or avoid setting limits out of a sense of guilt can raise manipulative children. Acknowledge your contribution to the problems in the marriage and learn from your mistakes. If you are feeling intense guilt, ask yourself, "If my best friend did what I feel so guilty about, what would I say to him or her?" Chances are, you're much harder on yourself than you would be to your friend. Keeping a journal is a good way to work through guilt because it can help you understand your feelings, concerns, and successes. Try writing something in it every day but do not share it with your children.

5: Venturing Forth Again

Summon the courage to try new relationships. Allow yourself to venture forth and start new relationships without guilt. Find someone who shares common interests with you. Get out and meet people by going dancing or taking a dance class. Go to parties. Find out if any athletic clubs cater to single people. Join a toastmasters or singles card club. Get to know people by volunteering your time. Establish

relationships that are built on realistic understanding and appreciation of one another as individuals.

6: Rebuilding

Develop new, better, healthy relationships that will include your
children and work on creating a life outside of marriage. Feel confident in your ability to cope with problems of daily living.

7: Helping the Children

Start to see the other parent as a person with strengths and
weaknesses and with whom you share a common commitment to
raise emotionally healthy children. Ingrid Bergman once said, "Happiness is good health and a bad memory. " Let go of the past and
focus on the future.

Changing Your Negative Thinking

William James said, "The greatest discovery of my generation is that
a human being can alter his life by altering his attitude." How then
do we change our attitude? Aaron Beck, father of cognitive behavioral therapy, discovered that we can change our feelings by changing how we think. The average person thinks fifty thousand thoughts
a day. Most of these thoughts are automatic and rarely noticed, but
have the power to create intense feelings. For example, let's say your
children's other parent takes your children to the zoo. If your thought
about this is, "I'm glad he is finally doing something that the children
enjoy," your feeling is going to be one of relief or pleasure. If, on the
other hand, your thought is, "He is always trying to outdo me. I'm so
sick of him being the Disneyland Dad and I get stuck making them
do their homework and chores," your feeling is going to be anger. If
we want to change how we feel, we need to change what we think.

There are many different names for these very powerful
thoughts that influence how we feel. Some call them the little voice in
the back of your head. I refer to them as your self-talk. If your little
voice or your self-talk is positive, you will tend to enjoy life. If the
voice is negative, life will be more difficult. Matthew McKay, Peter
Rogers, Joan Blades, and Richard Gosse, in *The Divorce Book*, refer to
unrealistic and inaccurate thoughts as "cognitive traps." They found
that many divorcing people increase their pain by falling into these

cognitive traps—habitual thoughts that raise anxiety, depression, and anger during divorce. These judgments and labels cause us to dwell on loss, danger, or injustice and create depression, anxiety, or rage.

To assess whether you are experiencing the cognitive traps of divorce, complete the following exercise, created by the authors of *The Divorce Book.*

EXERCISE 21: DIVORCE AWARENESS SCALE

Put an X in the box by any items that reflect how you think or feel.

- ❏ A1. A lot of people will be upset that I'm divorcing.
- ❏ A2. She/he was a loser.
- ❏ A3. I'll always be alone and lonely.
- ❏ A4. I've wasted my life.
- ❏ A5. I didn't love enough.
- ❏ A6. I should be turned on to this new freedom more than I am.
- ❏ A7. I was too good for him/her.
- ❏ A8. I'll no longer fit into my circle of friends.
- ❏ B1. His/her relatives will hate me. They'll blame me for hurting him/her.
- ❏ B2. She/he is a bitch, jerk, or _____ hole.
- ❏ B3. I'll never find anyone else.
- ❏ B4. I can't stand this loneliness.
- ❏ B5. If I'd only worked harder at it, I could have kept the marriage together.
- ❏ B6. I should be going out with a lot of people.
- ❏ B7. If she/he would have done a little changing, improved and compromised, or had been more accepting, things would have turned out differently.
- ❏ B8. I'm not going to survive financially.
- ❏ C1. Secretly, people will look down on me now.
- ❏ C2. She/he was basically selfish.
- ❏ C3. My relationships will always fail.
- ❏ C4. I'm overwhelmed by unbearable pain.
- ❏ C5. I wasn't a good husband/wife.

❑ C6. Even through I don't feel like it, I should be initiating contact. I should be asking people (of the opposite sex) out.

❑ C7. She/he made me miserable and ruined our marriage.

❑ C8. My ex-spouse will fall apart without me.

❑ D1. My friends won't want to see me.

❑ D2. She/he was stupid, insensitive, and/or inconsiderate.

❑ D3. Nobody will be attracted enough to me to want a relationship.

❑ D4. The hurt is too great.

❑ D5. If only I hadn't (*whatever you think you did*), everything would have been all right.

❑ D6. I shouldn't go out at night and abandon my kids.

❑ D7. His/her lack of communication had a lot to do with our divorce.

❑ D8. I'm not going to be able to stand this; I'll fall apart.

❑ E1. People blame me for the breakup.

❑ E2. She/he was mean, hostile, and/or sadistic.

❑ E3. I'll probably always feel depressed.

❑ E4. I spent my youth on him/her.

❑ E5. I messed up what could have been a good marriage.

❑ E6. I should have stayed married for the kids.

❑ E7. His/her hostility ruined things.

❑ E8. My children may be permanently harmed by the divorce.

❑ F1. People think I'm a failure.

❑ F2. She/he is a liar.

❑ F3. I'll never feel really close to anyone again.

❑ F4. I'm trapped and powerless.

❑ F5. I keep regretting the way I was and the mistakes I made in the marriage.

❑ F6. I shouldn't have hurt him/her. I should have worked harder to keep us together.

❑ F7. If she/he had worked harder, we could have saved the marriage.

❑ F8. I'm not going to be able to get back into dating or fit into modern single life.

❏ G1. My married friends don't understand. They feel uncomfortable around me.

❏ G2. She/he was withdrawn, uninvolved, and/or uncaring.

❏ G3. I'll never succeed in a marriage.

❏ G4. I feel like a failure.

❏ G5. I keep thinking that I'm responsible for the pain she/he is suffering.

❏ G6. I should be closer to people, more outgoing.

❏ G7. She/he never had enough time or paid enough attention to me. She/he didn't really care.

❏ G8. I'll have to live the rest of my life alone.

❏ H1. His/her friends secretly don't like me.

❏ H2. She/he was lousy at communication.

❏ H3. I'll never feel really secure again.

❏ H4. The anxiety and fear is overwhelming. I feel like I'm falling apart.

❏ H5. I wasn't flexible enough. I could have saved the marriage.

❏ H6. I should be independent and comfortable being alone.

❏ H7. I wasn't treated fairly. I was basically "screwed over."

❏ H8. New relationships will fail and I'll be hurt again.

Instructions for scoring the Divorce Awareness Scale.
This test has eight subscales. Follow the directions for scoring each one.
Subscale 1: Count the marked boxes for all number-one questions (A1, B1, C1, etc.).
     Total _____

Subscale 2: Count the marked boxes for all number-two questions (A2, B2, C2, etc.).
     Total _____

Subscale 3: Count the marked boxes for all number-three questions (A3, B3, C3, etc.).
     Total _____

Subscale 4: Count the marked boxes for all number-four questions (A4, B4, C4, etc.).
     Total _____

Subscale 5: Count the marked boxes for all number-five questions (A5, B5, C5, etc.).

Total _____

Subscale 6: Count the marked boxes for all number-six questions (A6, B6, C6, etc.).

Total _____

Subscale 7: Count the marked boxes for all number-two and number-seven questions (A2, A7, B2, B7, C2, C7, etc.).

Total _____

Subscale 8: Count the marked boxes for all number-three and number-eight questions (A3, A8, B3, B8, C3, C8, etc.).

Total _____

Scores for subscales 1 through 6 range between zero and eight. Scores for subscales 7 and 8 range between zero and sixteen. Elevated scores on a subscale suggest a tendency toward the cognitive trap tested by the subscale.

Subscale 1: Mind Reading

Higher scores on this scale indicate a tendency to make assumptions about the feelings, attitudes, and motivations of others—all without any direct confirmation. The divorcing person will often use mind reading to guess the reactions of relatives and friends. This becomes a special problem when you're afraid to hear the truth, one way or the other. You assume the worst, anticipating disapproval and rejection. You expect to be hurt, so you pull away or become defensive. This is the beginning of a self-fulfilling prophecy: your expectations may soon become reality.

In a survey of divorced people (McKay et al. 1984), one-fourth agreed with the statement, "Secretly people will look down on me now." This is a dangerous thought that can lead to significant anxiety and depression. You feel a loss of self-worth and expect to be shunned.

The best way to deal with mind reading is to commit yourself to making no inferences about people whatsoever. Either accept what they tell you or assume nothing at all until there is some conclusive evidence. Treat all your assumptions about people as hypotheses to be tested by asking them. Sit down with family and friends and find out, individually, how they are reacting to your divorce.

Subscale 2: Global Labeling

Higher scores on this scale indicate your tendency to generalize one or two negative qualities into a global judgment. The label ignores all contrary evidence in favor of a stereotyped, one-dimensional viewpoint. The trouble with labels is that they turn people into things. Instead of a complex, many-sided person, you see the personification of a single negative quality. Global labels fuel your rage. It's much easier to reject someone when he or she is "selfish" or "a loser" than it is when you see the whole person.

This divorce subscale focuses on labels that attack others. You can also do tremendous damage to your own self-esteem by applying global labels to yourself. In the McKay study, one-third of the respondents agreed with the statement, "I'm a loser because I got a divorce." Labeling yourself as a loser, a failure, or a jerk is the kind of self-rejection that can only deepen your depression.

The result of labeling is very simple: negative labels attached to others make you angry and disgusted. The same labels attached to yourself cause guilt and a sense of worthlessness.

The antidote for global labeling is limiting your description of others (and yourself) to specific behaviors. Your ex-wife is not a bitch. She just tends to become angry when negotiating child support. You are not a loser. You are a person who has gone through a divorce and feels the effects of emotional trauma. If you ban global labeling from your vocabulary, you'll find yourself less angry at others and less disgusted with yourself.

Subscale 3: Overgeneralizing

Higher scores indicate a tendency to make broad, generalized conclusions based on a single case or very little evidence. When you overgeneralize, you make absolute statements that imply immutable laws limiting your chances for happiness. The key words are: *all, every, never, always, everybody, none, nobody, totally,* and *continually.*

Overgeneralizations tend to defeat and frighten you. When you say to yourself, "I'll *always* feel depressed," you're depressing yourself even more. When you say, "I'll never feel secure again," you're increasing your fear. Notice how the words *always* and *never* add so much more negativity to the statement. Saying "I feel insecure" is one thing, but saying "I'll *never* feel secure" is condemning yourself to a lifetime of pain.

One-quarter of the divorced people in the McKay study agreed with the statements, "I'll *always* be alone" and "I'll *never* find anyone else." These statements tend to paralyze and defeat their victims. And they can become self-fulfilling prophecies. Since you don't expect to meet anyone, you may not bother to look.

Some generalizations undermine your relationships. Statements such as, "No man can be trusted," "All women are possessive," "Men only want sex," or "Women are out for the bucks" close you off to the opposite sex.

You can fight the tendency to overgeneralize by banishing the key words from your vocabulary. You can also fight this tendency by examining how much evidence you really have for your conclusions. If the conclusion is based on one or two cases, or merely on the feeling that it must be true, then throw it out until you have more convincing proof. Avoid absolutes. Admit the exceptions and the shades of gray; use words such as *sometimes, may,* or *often.*

Subscale 4: Filtering

Higher scores indicate a tendency to focus on the worst possible aspects of a situation and ignore everything else. Because filtering creates a kind of negative tunnel vision, the divorcing person will often magnify and "awfulize" his or her fears and losses. When you filter, you ignore the sunshine and look at the clouds. You magnify your fears and losses until they fill your awareness to the exclusion of everything else. Key words for filters are *terrible, awful,* and *horrible.* Key phrases are "can't stand it," "falling apart," and "completely overwhelmed." When you magnify in this way, your anxiety or depression will tend to skyrocket.

One-quarter of the respondents in the McKay survey agreed with the statement, "I've wasted my life." This is a perfect example of filtering. From a lifetime of ups and downs only the downs are remembered. The pain of divorce erases every happy memory.

To stop filtering, you have to stop thoughts such as, "I can't stand it" and "This is terrible, horrible." The truth is you *can* stand it. History shows that human beings can endure almost any psychological blow. You can survive and cope with almost anything. Instead of saying, "I can't stand it," use phrases such as, "There's no need to magnify," and "I can cope." Filters also need to shift their focus. You can do this in two ways. First, you can put your attention on coping strategies that deal with the problem rather than obsessing about the problem itself. Second, you can change your mental themes. If your theme is danger, you need to refocus on the things in your life that represent comfort and safety. If your theme is loss, concentrate on what you do have that you value. If your theme is injustice ("I've been screwed"), shift your attention to the ways you have been treated fairly.

Subscale 5: Self-Blame

Higher scores indicate a tendency to exaggerated responsibility for a spouse's pain and the breakup of the marriage. You perceive whatever happened as largely your fault. There is an inclination toward self-attack for mistakes, insensitivity, failing to work harder or love more, and so on. People who experience this cognitive trap feel the weight of the world on their shoulders. They have to right all wrongs, fill every need, and salve each hurt. If they don't, they feel guilty.

In the McKay study, one-third of divorced people agreed with the statement, "I didn't love enough." One-fifth believed, "If only I hadn't (fill in the blank), everything would have been all right." These statements are ideal for generating guilt. They leave you with all the responsibility for the breakup and ignore the interactive nature of every relationship.

Blaming yourself for your ex-spouse's problems is a form of self-aggrandizement. Basically you are saying, "I'm more responsible for your life than you are . . . I have more control of your happiness than you have . . . you're helpless without me." The truth is that your ex-spouse bears equal responsibility for the outcome of your marriage. Each of you must accept the consequences of your choices. By taking all the blame, you're turning your spouse into a child who depends on you for everything. You are denying his or her adulthood.

Subscale 6: Shoulds

Higher scores indicate a tendency to have strict rules governing what are acceptable thoughts, feelings, and actions. These rules often contradict what is healthy, natural, and needed at a particular stage in the divorce process. Cue words indicating the presence of this cognitive trap are *should, ought,* or *must.*

The problem with "should" is that you often feel compelled to do or not do things despite your genuine needs to the contrary. One-third of the people surveyed reported, "Even though I don't feel like it, I *should* be asking people out." Another third agreed with the statement, "I *should* be turned on to this new freedom more than I am." These "shoulds" may force you into doing something that could be inappropriate at your point in the divorcing process. For example, you may not be ready to go out yet. Forcing yourself to cash in on the "new freedom" may cut short the very essential mourning process.

The antidote for "shoulds" is to avoid using the words *should, ought,* or *must.* Use flexible rules and expectations that always admit exceptions and special circumstances. For example, telling yourself, "I should be independent and comfortable being alone," is like putting yourself inside a psychological straitjacket. You may end up denying important needs for security because you're stuck with an inflexible rule. It's better to say, "I would like to learn how to become more independent," or, "I hope to feel more comfortable alone." These statements admit that you're in a process and don't have to achieve your goals instantly. You may be more comfortable being alone in five months or five years. But right now it's okay to depend on others. Using the word *should* forces you to make premature and unhealthy demands on yourself.

Subscale 7: Blaming Others

Higher scores indicate a tendency to hold others responsible for any pain, loss, or failure. Your spouse is blamed for your loneliness, hurt, and fear. Blaming others has its roots in the belief that you are helpless to provide for your own emotional needs. You are a victim of the selfishness and insensitivity of others.

Blaming others keeps you from having to face your part in the breakup. As long as you focus on the failings of your ex-spouse, you can be protected from the awareness of your own failings. As long as you are angry, you don't have to be depressed. In the Divorce Awareness Scale, blaming also includes the use of global labels. Reducing your ex-spouse to a "bitch" or a "jerk" absolves you of any fault. He or she was bad and you are good.

In the McKay survey, one-third of the respondents agreed with the statements, "She/he made me miserable and ruined our marriage" and "I was too good for him/her." These statements fuel your anger and will make it harder to cooperate if you continue to share parenting.

The antidote for blaming is to focus on your own choices. You chose to marry your ex-spouse, and you endured, for a time, an unhappy marriage. You chose characteristic ways of dealing with your mate and solving problems. These choices are your responsibility. And the pain you lived with must also be, in some measure, your responsibility.

Subscale 8: Catastrophizing

Higher scores indicate a tendency to exaggerate potential danger. You habitually focus on future scenarios of disaster. The divorcing person may use this cognitive trap to plan a future full of bleak and frightening possibilities. Catastrophic thoughts often start with the words "what if": "What if I'm rejected by my friends?" "What if my children are damaged?" "What if I have to live the rest of my life alone?" These are frightening thoughts. The more airtime you give them, the more your anxiety grows.

In the Divorce Awareness Scale, catastrophizing includes overgeneralizing. "I'll never succeed in a marriage" is an unrealistic catastrophic fantasy. By saying *never*, you are falsely assuming that each new relationship must follow the same pattern.

In the survey of divorced people, one-quarter of the respondents reported believing, "I'm not going to be able to stand this." Such catastrophic thoughts tend to increase an already high level of anxiety. Financial concerns may also lead to catastrophizing. One-quarter of respondents agreed with the statement, "I'm not going to survive financially." Divorce often begets serious financial problems, but almost everyone *survives*. Questioning your survival heightens your anxiety and inhibits problem solving.

Notice that catastrophic statements always focus on the future. Things are going to get worse; disaster is right around the bend. By envisioning a future full of danger and pain, you suffer anxiety in the process.

To end catastrophizing you must give up the "what ifs." Instead, think in terms of percent probability. Are the chances one in a million, one in a thousand, or one in a hundred? During the day, write down your worries when they are most intense and rate the percent probability that the catastrophe will come true. At night, go over the day's list of worries and rate the percent probability now that you are comfortably ensconced in bed. Seeing a disaster that was inevitable at three o'clock become unlikely at eleven helps distance you from the power of your catastrophic thoughts.

The opposite of catastrophizing can also be a problem. Some people nurture unreal expectations of life after divorce. They imagine being rescued by a new relationship. They fantasize about meeting the white knight or goddess. They anticipate exciting sex and stimulating people. The result of unrealistic expectations is often bitter disappointment. The knight never arrives, the sex is unfulfilling, and the new relationship may bear a strange resemblance to the old.

Once you have begun to recognize your patterns of mind reading, global labeling, overgeneralizing, filtering, self-blame, shoulds, blaming others, and catastrophizing, you can begin to stop these negative thoughts and change them to more realistic productive ones. Once you have begun to recognize your cognitive traps, you can begin to change your self-talk. The next exercise will help you turn your negative, unrealistic, and inaccurate self-talk into more positive reality-based self-talk.

EXERCISE 22: CHANGING THE LITTLE VOICE IN THE BACK OF YOUR HEAD: CREATING YOUR OWN POSITIVE AFFIRMATIONS

The first part of changing your self-talk is to recognize what kinds of messages you give yourself.

Step 1: For one week, concentrate on and write down what you say to yourself. Listen to the voice in the back of your head.

Step 2: Take a yellow highlighter and mark negative comments you have made to yourself. Look for statements that start with "I can't....," "I don't deserve...," "I'm such a...," "I should have...," "I could have...," or "I would have..." Watch for unrealistic irrational beliefs and generalizations such as "I always" or "I never." Notice patterns of mind reading, global labeling, overgeneralizing, filtering, self-blame, shoulds, blaming others, or catastrophizing. After you have become aware of your negative thinking patterns, change them to more positive ones.

Step 3: Make a written list of positive affirming statements. Jack Canfield, self-esteem expert, outlines the following guidelines for positive affirmations.

- Begin your affirmations with a positive statement: "I can ..., I am ..., or I deserve ..."

- State the affirmation as if it is already happening: "I am a loving parent."

- Keep the statement short, simple, and specific. Using an "-ing" word such as "caring" helps.

- Incorporate your strengths.

- Choose action words.

- Include positive feeling words such as happy, proudly, peaceful, relaxed.

- Affirmations need to involve something over which you have control. Since you don't have control over the other parent, do not include them in your affirmations. Instead of saying, "My ex makes me so mad," say, "I am expressing my feelings in healthy, helpful ways."

Step 4. Once you have designed an affirmation, close your eyes and repeat it several times.

Step 5. Write the affirmations on sticky notes and place them around the house. (Warn your children ahead of time that you are doing this as they may wonder why you are wallpapering the house in this way. Explain to them that you are working on feeling better about yourself.)

Step 6. Whenever you have a negative thought about yourself, stop the thought and replace it with a positive affirmation. If you hear that little voice saying, "I'm a terrible parent. I'm always yelling at Jennie," say, "I put a note in Sabrina's lunch today. When she reads it she'll know I love her."

Step 7. Focus on what you do well as a parent and correct the mistakes you make rather than verbally beat yourself up about them.

Don't Believe Everything You Hear

Eleanor Roosevelt was quoted as saying, "No one can make you feel inferior without your permission." If your child's other parent criticizes you, it will only affect your self-esteem if you accept what is said as the truth. If someone says, "You let those kids get away with murder," say to yourself, " I set priorities with my children. I choose when to discipline them." When the other parent puts you down, respond by saying something positive to yourself. Use the list of affirmations in Exercise 20 from the previous chapter to replace negative thoughts with positive ones. Don't give others the power to determine how you feel about yourself.

Join a Support Group

Another source of support can come from joining a support group. Divorce support groups consist of other adults going through divorce. Group members can help each other accept that their feelings are normal and help each other cope with these feelings. Helping others who are going through divorce can also build your self-esteem. Some programs follow a step-by-step process or use speakers to aid in healing. Groups vary in age range and group number. Find a group that best suits your style and with whom you can feel comfortable sharing your feelings. You can find support groups through local churches or in your local newspapers. Community mental health centers, hospitals, and family therapy clinics often have listings of local support groups.

If you continue to experience intense long-lasting feelings of anger, sadness, guilt, or fear, you may want to consult with a professional therapist. The next chapter will help you determine if you need to see a therapist and will assist you in finding one.

On the Cyber Nation International, Inc. website where I located many of the quotes in this book, it is noted that when Thomas Edison died a friend found a note in his desk that read, "When you're down in the mouth, think of Jonah in the Whale. He came out all right." Millions of others all over the world have survived the pain of divorce. And just as you survived the loss of your first childhood pet or your first love—even though at the time you didn't think you would—you will make it through this too. As you work through your grief, you will discover that your pain becomes more manageable and life continues to be full of opportunities for growth and fulfillment.

13

Therapy

KEY POINTS

- If you or your children are in danger of hurting yourself or others, immediately seek the advice of a professional.
- Therapy can assist you and your children in coping with the divorce.
- If symptoms of depression, anxiety, or confusion do not subside, you or your children may need therapy.

When I first started providing therapy, some of the children that I worked with called me a "shrink." I'm happy to say that now I'm more often referred to as their "worry doctor," because I help them with their worries. Attitudes have changed and therapy is no longer seen as something that only mentally ill people need. When I went to my high school reunion many of my former classmates, after finding out that I had become a therapist, told me that they had been in therapy and felt it had been a positive experience. People from all walks of life and of various ethnic and socioeconomic groups seek out the assistance of a therapist. In fact, most of the clients I see in my practice are normal people who are having difficulty coping with a particular life stressor or change. They are usually having some problems at work or school or in their relationships with family or friends. Many are feeling depressed or anxious, or their behavior is causing problems at home or in the community.

Therapy is a process in which the therapist guides you through the process of recovery. Therapy can help you move past old hurts and negative memories to achieve healing. It can help build your self-esteem and assist you in discovering new meaning and value in your life. Therapy can help you find the courage to take risks. Therapists use a variety of treatment approaches in assisting you in finding your own answers and solutions to your problems. A session with a therapist usually lasts fifty minutes, and the number of sessions varies depending on your needs and the style of the therapist. Many therapists specialize in short-term therapy that lasts less than ten sessions. Most therapists will initially meet with you once a week, with a decrease over time as you make progress in your therapy.

Some people call therapists "counselors." I prefer the word *therapist* because I see therapy as a process: therapy has a beginning, middle, and end. At the first session, the therapist usually will discuss fees and ask you about your personal history and the reason you are seeking therapy. Confidentiality should also be discussed. I tell children that confidentiality is kind of like a one-way secret. The therapist is not allowed to discuss anything that you talk about in the session to anyone, without your written consent. You, however, can talk to anyone you choose or no one about what was discussed. The therapist may break this confidence only if he or she suspects child abuse or neglect or if he or she thinks that you are in danger of killing yourself or someone else. At the initial and subsequent sessions you and the therapist will identify short- and long-term goals for therapy. The therapist may ask you to sign a contract that outlines these goals.

As therapy progresses you will discuss your feelings and thoughts in greater detail. The therapist will ask you how long the problems that you have identified have existed. You will talk about who is involved in the problems and how you have previously coped. You and the therapist will then work toward a positive outcome to these problems. The therapist may, instead of focusing on problems, assist you in identifying the things that you already do to help yourself and support you in doing more of what is already working for you. To facilitate the process of recovery, the therapist may also give you homework assignments to complete between sessions. When you and the therapist decide that you are ready to end therapy you will discuss how to maintain the changes that you have made.

Therapy for Your Children

If you are concerned about your child's expression of feelings or if your child is having difficulty coping with the divorce, consider taking him or her to a therapist. Therapy can provide an opportunity for your children to accept, understand, and express their feelings. The therapist can assess your child's need for individual, group, or family therapy. Individual therapy involves one-on-one sessions between the therapist and your child. In family therapy, other family members, including siblings, participate in the session. With group therapy, other children with similar problems and usually within the same age range meet as a group to talk about a specific problem. The therapist in group sessions serves as a facilitator to these discussions. Some schools or family service agencies offer divorce groups for children. Divorce groups can assist children in alleviating shame and in understanding that they are not alone.

"When I first suggested to Tammy that I take her to see a counselor, she said, 'Why do I need to go see some head shrinker? You think I'm crazy!' I told her that I knew she wasn't crazy but that I thought it would help to have someone to talk to about how difficult the divorce had been for her. I let her know that I wanted her to at least meet the therapist and then if she didn't want to go back I wouldn't force her. She said she'd go but she wasn't going to say anything. I told her that was okay. After the first session, she agreed to go back and continued to see the therapist for about four months. She never talked about what went on in her sessions but I noticed a change in her behavior. She wasn't as moody anymore and her grades in school got better. And when her dad didn't show up for his visit she called a friend to do something rather than moping around the house for hours waiting for him to show up" (Martha, mother of a fourteen-year-old). Some children, particularly adolescents, may resist seeing a therapist. Focusing on their need for solutions to the problems that are causing their pain and stress may spark their interest. If a child is resisting treatment, I usually suggest to parents that the child come to one session. Usually the resistance decreases once the child meets the therapist and experiences the nonjudgmental response from the therapist.

"I don't know why I'm paying ninety dollars an hour for Jenny to play house" (Ed, father of a ten-year-old). Therapy for children, particularly young children, is different than therapy for adults in that the therapist may spend much of the time playing, coloring, or reading to your child. Children express themselves through their play, so the therapist may use therapeutic play to help your children work through their issues. For example, Jenny was unable to talk about how she felt about her parents' divorce. I used doll play to help her express her feelings about it. Jenny would say to the father doll as she put him in another part of the playroom, "This is your new home." I would then talk to Jenny about how the girl and boy doll felt about their father moving out. Although Jenny was unable to talk directly about how she felt about the divorce, she was able to talk about how the girl and boy doll felt. When I asked her what the girl and boy dolls could do to feel better, she acted out the girl doll calling the father doll on the telephone to tell him that she missed him. Jenny then placed the father doll in a toy car and drove it over to the dollhouse to take the children dolls out to dinner.

"Will my ex-husband or I be included in my son's treatment?" (Janice, mother of a seven-year-old). Therapists differ in how involved they expect the parents to be. A family therapist may expect all family members to attend and participate in every session. Other therapists may meet with the parents separately from the child. Discuss with the therapist what your role will be and policies about how much information will be shared with you about what takes place during the individual sessions with the child. Communicate with your former partner that your child is in therapy and provide him or her with the therapist's name and telephone number.

To find out if your child needs therapy, complete the next exercise.

EXERCISE 23: DOES MY CHILD NEED THERAPY?

If your child has made an attempt to physically harm herself, immediately consult with a professional therapist. Many communities have twenty-four-hour mental-health hotlines especially for adolescents. If you can not locate one, call 911 or contact the local hospital emergency center.

If you answer yes to any of the questions below, you should take your child to a professional child therapist for an evaluation.

1. Do I think my child is going to hurt himself?
   Does my child talk about killing himself?
   Does my child talk about wanting to die?
   Has my child tried to hurt himself in the past?

2. Is my child using alcohol or drugs?

3. Is my child deliberately starting fires?

4. Is my child engaging in delinquent activities (i.e., stealing, damaging property, assault)?

5. Has my child run away?

6. Is my child being physically or sexually abused?

7. Is my child physically cruel to animals or people?

8. Is my child refusing to go to school, I'm unable to get him or her to go?

9. Has my child lost over 15 percent of her body weight below what is normal for her age and height?

10. Does my child binge eat on a recurrent basis, followed by self-induced vomiting, or use laxatives, diuretics, strict dieting, or fasting in order to prevent weight gain?

Consider taking your child to a therapist if you answer yes to any of the following questions:

1. Have friends or family members suggested that my child needs counseling?

2. Do school counselors, teachers, or health care providers suggest that I take my child to therapy?

3. Do I feel I need help outside of family and friends to deal with my child's behavior?

4. Has my child expressed a desire to see a counselor?

Although many of the following symptoms are normal during a divorce or may arise as your child matures, consult with your child's school counselor or professional therapist if the following symptoms persist.

1. Have there been significant changes in my child's personality?

2. Is my child experiencing behavioral problems that are intense and frequent and do not change despite parental efforts to use rewards, consequences, or explanations?

   These include an increase in lying, breaking rules, manipulating parents against each other, refusing to take responsibility for his own problems, constantly blaming others, destroying property, or underachieving in school.

3. Is my child constantly avoiding playing with children his own age despite availability of same-age peers?

4. Does my child appear depressed?

   Does my child appear lethargic or overly tired?

   Does she resist getting up or going to school in the morning more often than she used to?

   Is my child having trouble concentrating at school? Does my child appear more irritable than normal?

   Is my child isolating himself from family and friends?

   Does my child view the future as totally hopeless?

   Has my child lost interest in the activities that she normally enjoys doing?

   Have there recently been major changes in my child's eating or sleeping patterns?

   Is my child having difficulty falling asleep at night or sleeping more than normal?

5. Does my child appear overly anxious and worried?

   Has my child started wetting his pants after displaying continence for over one year?

   Has my child recently started excessive nail-biting, nose-picking, stuttering, or has she displayed other repetitive nervous habits?

Does my child experience persistent and excessive or unrealistic worry about future events?

Is my child continually complaining of physical symptoms (i.e., headaches, stomachaches), despite the pediatrician finding nothing wrong?

Does my child experience persistent, excessive, and unrealistic worry about me?

6. Is my child acting out her feelings toward one particular member of the household? (For example, excessive teasing or name calling, hitting, spitting, biting, throwing things)

7. Does my child frequently lose his temper?

8. Is my child feeling:
   Torn between his mother and father?
   Alone or isolated?
   Uncomfortable with any member of her biological or stepfamily?
   Intense and long-lasting guilt, irritability, anger, or worry?

9. Is my child continually resisting parental authority?

10. Is my child experiencing frequent and intense nightmares?

11. Is my child terrified of being separated from me?

12. Is my child's self-esteem low?
    Is my child continually saying she hates herself or that she's no good?
    Does my child persistently say he's ugly, fat, or stupid?
    Does my child seem to always feel that nobody likes him or that nobody wants to be his friend?
    Does my child frequently and persistently experience excessive or unrealistic concern about her competence in the areas of sports, school, or friends?

13. Is my young child having difficulty expressing or receiving affection?

In the Personal Notes section at the back of this book, write down what you would like your child to get out of therapy.

Do I Need a Therapist?

"When I was first separated, I felt like my whole life had been turned upside down. I didn't know what was normal anymore. My neighbor suggested that I go talk to somebody. I didn't think I was that bad off but she assured me that a lot of normal people go see therapists and that she had seen one when she was going through her divorce. I decided to give it a try. I only went for a few months but it helped me make it through the rough spots" (Kendra, mother of three). Adults as well as children all have times when they feel depressed, anxious, or confused. Divorce is a loss for you and it is normal to grieve. Intense feelings of anger, sadness, and fear may at times feel so overwhelming that it feels like you are going crazy. Although the emotional roller coaster you are on is normal, you may need to seek the help of a professional therapist for yourself, particularly if symptoms of depression or anxiety do not start to diminish. Going through a divorce is a major life change and many divorcing men and women receive much needed support and guidance offered through therapy.

The next exercise will help you identify if you need a therapist.

EXERCISE 24: DO I NEED A THERAPIST?

If you answer yes to the following questions you should talk to a therapist.

1. Am I thinking about hurting myself?

2. Am I using alcohol or drugs to numb my feelings?

If you answer yes to more than one question in any of the following categories you should talk to a therapist.

1. Have friends or family members suggested that I seek counseling?
    Do friends or family tell me that they are worried about me?
    Do they suggest I see a therapist?

2. Am I trying to deal with the same old problems?
    Do I feel stuck?
    Do I find myself at night going over and over the same issues?

3. Do I feel anxious more days than not?
    Do I spend most of my time worrying about what

might happen?

Has my worry interfered with my ability to do my job?

Has my anxiety or worry affected my relationships with friends or family?

Has my anxiety or worry affected how well I am doing in school or my ability to parent?

4. Do I like myself?

Am I my own worst enemy?

Do I look in the mirror and pick apart the way I look?

Am I constantly comparing myself to others and feeling less adequate than they are?

Do I feel like crying or punching someone every time someone criticizes me?

Do I see myself as a total failure?

Do I believe that no one does or will ever love me?

Do I constantly need for others to admire and praise me?

Do I think that I have to have sex with someone to be liked?

5. Do I feel depressed, sad, or empty?

Do I wake up more days than not thinking I can't face the day?

Am I finding it impossible to make everyday decisions?

Do I see the future as totally hopeless?

Do I think I cannot take care of my children or myself?

Have I lost interest in the activities I normally enjoy doing?

6. Have there recently been major changes in my eating or sleeping patterns?

Have I gained or lost more than 15 percent of my body weight in the past month?

Am I having difficulty falling asleep most nights?

Am I sleeping more and using sleep to escape from life?

Have I been unsuccessful at numerous attempts to improve my sleeping habits on my own?

7. Am I burying myself in my work?

Do I devote all of my time to work and being productive?

Am I constantly avoiding spending time in leisure activities and hobbies I used to enjoy?

Am I working instead of being with friends?

Consider seeing a therapist who specializes in stepfamily issues if any of the following are true.

> 8. I have remarried and I am (or my spouse is) feeling resentment because:
> One parent openly favors one of the children.
> One parent is doing all of the discipline.

In the Personal Notes section at the back of this book, write down any thoughts, feelings, or behaviors you can think of that you would like to change in therapy.

Finding a Qualified Therapist

"I knew my son Brandon was having a hard time with the divorce but when he started skipping school and hanging out with some troubled kids, I knew I needed to do something. I didn't know where to begin. It just didn't feel right to look up some stranger's name in the phone book like I was hiring someone to fix my dryer, so I called my son's school counselor. Mr. Brown, who was also my son's wrestling coach, gave me the names of a few therapists and I called to find out if any of them took our insurance. I think Brandon agreed to go because Mr. Brown had told him that he trusted this guy. It helped me feel less anxious knowing that another professional was familiar with his work" (Carolyn, mother of four). If you are looking for a therapist for your children, find one who has experience working with children of divorce. If the therapist is for yourself, make sure he or she has experience working with adults going through divorce. Make sure the therapist is licensed or registered and has a master's or doctoral degree in social work, psychology, or counseling. To find a qualified therapist check with your child's school social worker or counselor, the employee assistance program (EAP) at your workplace, or ask your minister, priest, or friends to recommend someone. Look in the yellow pages under "Family Therapy Clinics." If finances are a problem, ask the therapist or agency if they charge according to sliding fee scales based on your income. Check to see if your insurance plan covers therapy, and if it does find out what percentage of the fee they pay. If you have an EAP at work, check to see what it offers. Sometimes your insurance will cover a greater portion of the therapy if you get a referral from your EAP. If you are calling a family service agency, ask the clinical director which therapists specialize in working with adults or children of divorce.

Ask the therapist, either on the phone or at the first session, the following questions.

1. What are your areas of expertise?

2. What kind of training do you have?

3. How often do you treat children going through divorce (or other problem for which you are seeking help)?

4. What is your approach to treatment?

5. How do you define recovery?

6. What will be my role in treatment?

7. What will be the role of my family in treatment?

8. What are your fees?

9. How often will we meet?

10. How long do you think this process will take?

I borrowed these words from the Serenity Prayer to sum up what therapy can do for you: Therapy can help you accept the things you cannot change, give you the courage to change the things you can, and develop the wisdom to know the difference.

Afterword

"The best way to predict the future is to invent it."
—Alan Kay

Being divorced presents you with an opportunity to re-exam your life and your dream of what you want your marriage and family to be. It demands that you look deep within yourself and draw on resources that you never knew you had. You have it within you to generate the courage, commitment, compassion, and communication it will take to make life for you and your children a full and growing experience.

To aid your family in looking forward to the future, create together a "Portrait of Our Future."

EXERCISE 25: PORTRAIT OF OUR FUTURE

Materials

1 poster board

Colored pencils, crayons, markers, or paints

Scissors

Glue sticks

Old magazines

Step 1. Sit down at a table or on a hard floor with all of your children. If you have remarried, also include your spouse and any stepchildren.

Step 2. Talk to your children about how much you are looking forward to your future as a family and tell them several specific things that you are looking forward to, such as the cookies you are planning to make together for next week's bake sale, your son's concert that all of you plan on attending at the end of the month, or the vacation you are planning next summer.

Step 3. Tell your children that together you are going to make a picture about your future together. Explain that each of you is going to take turns adding to the picture. Tell them they can write a word, draw a picture, or cut a picture out of a magazine that shows something that they are looking forward to doing as a family. Let them know that you'll go first to show them what you have in mind.

Step 4. In one corner of the paper draw a picture, write a word, or cut out and paste a picture from a magazine that illustrates what you are looking forward to doing together. For example, you could draw a picture of you and your children sitting together reading a story. You could also cut out a picture of a bicycle if you plan on bike riding as a family or just write the word *hopeful*.

Step 5. Have each of your children take turns adding to the picture.

Step 6. When it is you turn, you may want to vary the modality you used last turn. For example, if you drew a picture last turn of all of you camping, the next turn write the word *love*. However, don't ask your children to do something different each turn. Allow them to use whatever modality they are comfortable with. (If your children say they can't think of anything, ask them what they would like to do together. If they still resist, make a couple of suggestions of things you think they might enjoy.)

Step 7. Ask your children where they would like to hang the picture. Give each child a hug.

> *"Life affords no greater responsibility, no greater*
> *privilege, than the raising of the next generation."*
> —C. Everett Koop

Cherish the gift you have been given as a parent and take advantage of the opportunities that have been opened to you.

References, Bibliography, and Additional Reading

References

Kelly, Joan B. 1998. "Marital Conflict, Divorce and Children's Adjustment." Child and Adolescent Psychiatric Clinics of North America *Child Custody* 7(2).

McKay, Matthew et al. 1984. *The Divorce Book*. Oakland, Calif.: New Harbinger Publications.

Wallerstein, Judith. 1989. *2nd Chances: Men, Women, and Children a Decade after Divorce; Who Wins, Who Loses—and Why*. New York: Ticknor and Fields.

Wallerstein, Judith, and Joan Berlin Kelly. 1980. *Surviving the Breakup*. New York: Basic Books.

http://www.cyber-nation.com/victory/quotations/
Cyber Nation International, Inc., in Blaine, Washington, is a site that offers numerous quotations on various subjects.

Bibliography

Ahrons, Constance R. 1994. *The Good Divorce; Keeping Your Family Together When Your Marriage Comes Apart*. New York: Harper Collins Publishers.

Bennett, Steve, and Ruth Bennett. 1991. *365 TV-Free Activities You Can Do with Your Child*. Boston: Bob Adams.

Berger, Stuart. 1983. *Divorce Without Victims; Helping Children Through Divorce with a Minimum of Pain and Trauma*. Boston: Houghton Mifflin Company.

Bienefeld, Florence. 1987. *Helping Your Child Succeed after Divorce*. Claremont, Calif.: Hunter House.

Canfield, Jack. 1989. *Self-Esteem and Peak Performance, an Audio Cassette Seminar*. Boulder, Colo.: Career Track.

Carlson, Richard. 1997. *Don't Sweat the Small Stuff . . . and It's All Small Stuff*. New York: Hyperion.

Carnegie, Dale. 1981. *How to Win Friends and Influence People*. New York: Simon and Schuster.

Covey, Steven. 1989. *The 7 Habits of Highly Effective People*. New York: Simon and Schuster.

Gardner, Richard. 1977. *The Parents' Book about Divorce*. Garden City, NY: Doubleday and Company.

Gold, Lois. 1992. *Between Love and Hate: A Guide to Civilized Divorce*. New York: Plenum Press.

Kline, Kris, and Stephen Pew. 1992. *For the Sake of the Children, How to Share Your Children with Your Ex-Spouse in Spite of Your Anger.* Rocklin, Calif.: Prima Publishing.

Lansdy, Vicki. 1991. *101 Ways to Make Your Child Feel Special.* Chicago: Contemporary Books.

McKay, Matthew, and Patrick Fanning. 1992. *Self-Esteem.* Oakland, Calif.: New Harbinger Publications.

Neumann, Diane. 1989. *Divorce Mediation; How to Cut the Cost and Stress of Divorce.* New York: Henry Holt and Co.

Pearsall, Paul. 1987. *Super Immunity.* New York: Fawcett Gold Medal.

Pruett, Marsha Kline, and Kathy Hoganbruen. 1998. "Joint Custody and Shared Parenting; Research and Interventions." Child and Adolescent Psychiatric Clinics of North America, *Child Custody* 7(2).

Ross, Julie, and Judy Corcoran. 1996. *Joint Custody with a Jerk; Raising a Child with an Uncooperative Ex.* New York: St. Martin Press.

Shulman, Diana. 1996. *Co-Parenting after Divorce: How to Raise Happy, Healthy Children in Two-Home Families.* Sherman Oaks, Calif.: Winnspeed Press.

Smith, Judith, and Donald Smith. 1979. *Child Management: A Program for Parents and Teachers.* Champaign, Ill.: Research Press Company.

Troyer, Warner. 1979. *Divorce Kids.* New York: Harcourt Brace Jovanovich.

Additional Reading and Websites

Boegehold, Betty. 1985. *Daddy Doesn't Live Here Anymore; A Book About Divorce.* Racine, Wisc.: Western Pub. Co.

Brown, Laurene Kransy, and Marc Brown. 1986. *Dinosaur Divorce.* Boston: Antlantic Monthly Press.

Cook, Jean. 1995. *Room for a Stepdaddy.* Morton Grove, Ill.: A. Whitman.

Gardner, Richard. 1971. *The Boy's and Girl's Book about Divorce.* New York: Bantam.

Garigan and Urbanski. 1991. *Living with Divorce: Journal Activities for Personal Growth.* Carthage, Ill.: Good Apple.

Hogan, Paula. 1980. *Will Dad Ever Move Back Home?* Milwaukee, Wisc.: Raintree Children's Books.

Kimball, Gayle. 1994. *How to Survive Your Parents' Divorce: Kids Advice to Kids.* Chico, Calif.: Equality Press.

Krementz, Jill. 1988. *How it Feels When Parents Divorce.* New York: Random House.

Mayle, Peter. 1988. *Why Are We Getting a Divorce?* New York: Crown Publishers.

Prokop, Michael S. 1986. *Divorce Happens to the Nicest Kids.* Warren, Ohio: Alegra House.

Rogers, Fred. 1996. *Let's Talk About It: Divorce.* New York: Putnam's Sons.

Seuling, Barbara. 1985. *What Kind of Family Is This? A Book about Stepfamilies.* Racine, Wisc.: Western Pub.

Singergstenson, Janet. 1979. *Now I Have a Stepparent and It's Kind of Confusing.* New York: The Hearst Corporation.

Stinson, Kathy. 1984. *Mom and Dad Don't Live Together Anymore.* Toronto: Annick Press.

Websites

http://www.hec.ohio-state.edu/famlife/index.htm

This is a website for children ages twelve to fifteen who are going through divorce. Teens can get information, ask questions, or chat with other teens.

http://cosd.bayside.net/newsmed.htm

This is a website for the organization Children of Separation and Divorce (COSD) in Columbia, Maryland. This organization is aimed at helping families adjust to the process of separation, divorce, and remarriage.

http://www.divorce-online.com/

An information and referral source about divorce.

http://www.divorcesupport.com/index.html

A divorce information network.

http://www.divorcesource.com/

Provides information on child custody, child support, alimony, counseling, visitation, and legal processes.

http://www.positivesteps.com/

Provides research and support for stepfamilies.

http://stepparenting.miningco.com/

Net links and articles for stepparents.

http://divorcesupport.miningco.com/

Net links and articles for individuals going through divorce.

http://www.aacap.org/web/aacap/factsFam/

This site is a list of fact sheets provided by The American Academy of Child and Adolescent Psychiatry. Its goal is to educate parents about psychiatric disorders affecting children and adolescents.

Personal Notes and
To Do Lists

Introduction

What would you like to accomplish with the completion of this book?

_____

_____

_____

Other notes:

_____

_____

_____

Chapter 1

When do you plan to tell your children about the divorce, and/or when one parent will be moving out?

_____

What is your child-friendly explanation of why you are getting a divorce?

_____

_____

_____

What is your child-friendly explanation of how your love for your children is different from the love you had for your former partner?

_____

_____

_____

Write down anything you weren't able to finish discussing at your Family Meeting. Include anything that you need to follow up on, either alone with a child or at the next meeting.

_____

_____

_____

Other notes:

_____

_____

_____

Chapter 2

List of items for your child's "personal kit," which will travel back and forth between homes.

_____

_____

_____

_____

_____

_____

Is there anything else you can think of that will make the transition from one home to another easier?

_____

_____

Activities that you and your child enjoy doing together:

_____

_____

Ideas for communicating with your children when they are with their other parent:

_____

_____

Other notes:

_____

_____

_____

Chapter 3

Notes:

_____

_____

_____

_____

Chapter 4

Three instances in which your former partner did well in the parental role:

_____

_____

_____

What kind of relationship between you and your former partner would be most beneficial for your children?

_____

_____

List of names, addresses, and phone numbers of family and friends who love your children:

_____

_____

_____

_____

_____

Are there any questions you can think of that you would like to ask a mediator?

_____

_____

_____

Other notes:

_____

_____

_____

Chapter 5

Ideas you can think of to keep communication with the other parent open:

_____

_____

_____

What do you hear your children telling you about how the divorce is affecting them?

_____

_____

_____

Other notes:

_____

_____

_____

Chapter 6

List of things you do to cope with painful feelings:

_____

_____

_____

_____

Three positive things each of your children has done in the past week:

_____

_____

_____

Other notes:

_____

_____

_____

Chapter 7

Ways that you can help your infant cope with your divorce:

_____

_____

_____

Ways that you can help your toddler cope with your divorce:

_____

_____

_____

Ways that you can help your preschooler cope with your divorce:

_____

_____

_____

Ways that you can help your six-to-eight-year-old cope with your divorce:

_____

_____

_____

Ways that you can help your nine-to-twelve-year-old cope with your divorce:

_____

_____

_____

Ways that you can help your teenagers cope with your divorce:

_____

_____

_____

Ways that you can help your adult children cope with your divorce:

_____

_____

_____

Other notes:

_____

_____

_____

Chapter 8

What qualities are important to you in a relationship?

_____

_____

_____

_____

_____

If you are currently dating, which of the qualities listed above describe the person with whom you are involved?

_____

_____

_____

_____

Other notes:

_____

_____

_____

Chapter 9

Ideas for romantic things you can do for your spouse that are special and out of the ordinary:

_____

_____

_____

_____

_____

Other notes:

_____

_____

_____

Chapter 10

Ideas about what you can do to build your relationship with your stepchildren:

_____

_____

_____

_____

Ideas for new traditions you can start in your family:

_____

_____

_____

Ideas for spending time alone with your stepchildren:

_____

_____

_____

Other notes:

_____

_____

_____

Chapter 11

A list of peaceful calming things and places you can think about at bedtime to help you sleep:

_____

_____

_____

_____

_____

A few things you can do *this week* to reduce your stress:

_____

_____

_____

_____

Something you have accomplished today:

_____

_____

Other notes:

_____

_____

_____

Chapter 12

Something you have dreamed off doing but never did:

_____

_____

Three healthy things you can do when you are angry:

_____

_____

_____

Other notes:

_____

_____

_____

Chapter 13

What would you like your child to get out of therapy?

_____

_____

Thoughts, feelings, or behaviors you would like to change in therapy:

_____

_____

_____

Other notes:

_____

_____

_____

Some Other New Harbinger Self-Help Titles

Facing 30: Women Talk About Constructing a Real Life and Other Scary Rites of Passage, $12.95
The Worry Control Workbook, $15.95
Wanting What You Have: A Self-Discovery Workbook, $18.95
When Perfect Isn't Good Enough: Strategies for Coping with Perfectionism, $13.95
The Endometriosis Survival Guide, $13.95
Earning Your Own Respect: A Handbook of Personal Responsibility, $12.95
High on Stress: A Woman's Guide to Optimizing the Stress in Her Life, $13.95
Infidelity: A Survival Guide, $13.95
Stop Walking on Eggshells, $14.95
Consumer's Guide to Psychiatric Drugs, $16.95
The Fibromyalgia Advocate: Getting the Support You Need to Cope with Fibromyalgia and Myofascial Pain, $18.95
Healing Fear: New Approaches to Overcoming Anxiety, $16.95
Working Anger: Preventing and Resolving Conflict on the Job, $12.95
Sex Smart: How Your Childhood Shaped Your Sexual Life and What to Do About It, $14.95
You Can Free Yourself From Alcohol & Drugs, $13.95
Amongst Ourselves: A Self-Help Guide to Living with Dissociative Identity Disorder, $14.95
Healthy Living with Diabetes, $13.95
Dr. Carl Robinson's Basic Baby Care, $10.95
Better Boundaries: Owning and Treasuring Your Life, $13.95
Goodbye Good Girl, $12.95
Being, Belonging, Doing, $10.95
Thoughts & Feelings, Second Edition, $18.95
Depression: How It Happens, How It's Healed, $14.95
Trust After Trauma, $15.95
The Chemotherapy & Radiation Survival Guide, Second Edition, $14.95
Surviving Childhood Cancer, $12.95
The Headache & Neck Pain Workbook, $14.95
Perimenopause, $16.95
The Self-Forgiveness Handbook, $12.95
A Woman's Guide to Overcoming Sexual Fear and Pain, $14.95
Mind Over Malignancy, $12.95
Treating Panic Disorder and Agoraphobia, $44.95
Don't Take It Personally, $12.95
Becoming a Wise Parent For Your Grown Child, $12.95
Clear Your Past, Change Your Future, $13.95
Preparing for Surgery, $17.95
The Power of Two, $12.95
It's Not OK Anymore, $13.95
The Daily Relaxer, $12.95
The Body Image Workbook, $17.95
Living with ADD, $17.95
Taking the Anxiety Out of Taking Tests, $12.95
When Anger Hurts Your Kids, $12.95
The Addiction Workbook, $17.95
The Chronic Pain Control Workbook, Second Edition, $17.95
Fibromyalgia & Chronic Myofascial Pain Syndrome, $19.95
Flying Without Fear, $13.95
Kid Cooperation: How to Stop Yelling, Nagging & Pleading and Get Kids to Cooperate, $13.95
The Stop Smoking Workbook: Your Guide to Healthy Quitting, $17.95
Conquering Carpal Tunnel Syndrome and Other Repetitive Strain Injuries, $17.95
An End to Panic: Breakthrough Techniques for Overcoming Panic Disorder, Second Edition, $18.95
Letting Go of Anger: The 10 Most Common Anger Styles and What to Do About Them, $12.95
Messages: The Communication Skills Workbook, Second Edition, $15.95
Coping With Chronic Fatigue Syndrome: Nine Things You Can Do, $13.95
The Anxiety & Phobia Workbook, Second Edition, $18.95
The Relaxation & Stress Reduction Workbook, Fourth Edition, $17.95
Living Without Depression & Manic Depression: A Workbook for Maintaining Mood Stability, $18.95
Coping With Schizophrenia: A Guide For Families, $15.95
Visualization for Change, Second Edition, $15.95
Angry All the Time: An Emergency Guide to Anger Control, $12.95
Couple Skills: Making Your Relationship Work, $14.95
Self-Esteem, Second Edition, $13.95
I Can't Get Over It, A Handbook for Trauma Survivors, Second Edition, $16.95
Dying of Embarrassment: Help for Social Anxiety and Social Phobia, $13.95
The Depression Workbook: Living With Depression and Manic Depression, $17.95
Men & Grief: A Guide for Men Surviving the Death of a Loved One, $14.95
When Once Is Not Enough: Help for Obsessive Compulsives, $14.95
Beyond Grief: A Guide for Recovering from the Death of a Loved One, $14.95
Hypnosis for Change: A Manual of Proven Techniques, Third Edition, $15.95
When Anger Hurts, $13.95